Going Global for the Greater Good

Bonnie L. Koenig

Going Global for the Greater Good

Succeeding as a Nonprofit in the International Community

JOSSEY-BASS
A Wiley Imprint
www.josseybass.com

Published by Jossey-Bass
A Wiley Imprint
989 Market Street, San Francisco, CA 94103-1741   www.josseybass.com

Excerpts from "Training Your Staff to Think Internationally," by Bonnie Koenig, FORUM
magazine, March 2002, are used with permission.

Excerpts from "How Relevant Is Global Thinking," by Bonnie Koenig, *Nonprofit World*,
January-February 2001, and from "The Fine Art of Meeting Planning," by Bonnie Koenig,
Nonprofit World, November-December 1998, are used with permission from the Society for
Nonprofit Organizations, www.snpo.org.

Jossey-Bass books and products are available through most bookstores. To contact Jossey-Bass
directly call our Customer Care Department within the U.S. at 800-956-7739, outside the
U.S. at 317-572-3986, or fax 317-572-4002.

Jossey-Bass also publishes its books in a variety of electronic formats. Some content that
appears in print may not be available in electronic books.

Library of Congress Cataloging-in-Publication Data
Koenig, Bonnie L., 1957-
   Going global for the greater good: succeeding as a nonprofit in the
international community / by Bonnie L. Koenig.—1st ed.
        p. cm.
Includes bibliographical references and index.
   ISBN 0-7879-6676-2 (alk. paper) ·
   1. Nonprofit organizations—Management. 2. Strategic alliances
(Business) 3. International organization. 4. Globalization. I. Title.

HD62.6.K63 2004
658'.049—dc22

                                            2003027459

Printed in the United States of America
FIRST EDITION
HB Printing   10 9 8 7 6 5 4 3 2 1

Contents

Preface

The increase in the number of nongovernmental organizations (NGOs) that are operating at the international level is one of the most significant sector trends of the end of the twentieth century.[1] According to the *Global Civil Society 2002* report, "The decade of the 1990s had witnessed the spread of social movements, NGOs and citizens' networks across national boundaries. . . . Our figures showed a rapid growth in international NGOs during the last decade as well as a dramatic increase in parallel summits, and meetings of global civil society actors."[2] This growth was fueled by many factors, including two developments that took on major significance during the 1990s: the increased ease of global communications and increased face-to-face meetings helped in part by a series of conferences on social issues, sponsored by the United Nations (UN), that helped to facilitate network building.

The increased ease of global communications during the period, including the phenomenal growth of the Internet and e-mail, has been well documented. In the NGO community, it allowed grassroots and local organizations to communicate at the international level in a way that previously was not possible or was prohibitively expensive.

A series of UN-sponsored conferences on social issues also accelerated the growing awareness of NGOs of their role in the global arena. Starting in 1992 with the United Nations Conference on Environment and Development (UNCED, often referred to as the Earth Summit) in Rio de Janeiro, Brazil, the UN sponsored a series of conferences throughout the 1990s and into the new century that drew increasingly larger numbers of NGO representatives. Although the UN had sponsored such conferences in the past, the number of participants attending the conferences in the 1990s was at a vastly different scale than had ever attended before.

According to the UN's Department of Public Information, "The presence and influence of NGOs, one of the most active forces in the drive for gender equality, increased dramatically since [the first world conference on the status of women in] Mexico City in 1975. In Beijing [in 1995], NGOs directly influenced the content of the Platform for Action and they would play an important role in holding their national leaders accountable for the commitments they had made to implement the Platform."[3]

When the first world conference on the status of women was convened in Mexico City in 1975, 133 member state delegations gathered there. Women also organized a parallel NGO Forum, which attracted approximately four thousand participants.

The Beijing Conference twenty years later, in 1995, was the largest gathering of government and NGO representatives ever held, with seventeen thousand in attendance, including representatives of 189 governments. The NGO Forum held parallel to the conference also broke all records, bringing the combined number of participants to over forty-seven thousand.[4]

When these attendees returned home, many of them sustained the relationships they had made in these meetings, continuing to learn from and share information with colleagues around the world to support their own local work. These experiences also brought about a change in the approach of international organizations such as the United Nations toward NGOs. Kofi Annan, the secretary general of the United Nations beginning in 1997, was an important supporter of NGO involvement at the UN. Among his many statements of support was this one: "A true partnership between NGOs and the United Nations is not an option; it is a necessity."[5]

When they returned home from these conferences, many attendees were able to use rapidly expanding electronic resources to continue their networking in ways that had not been possible before. Web sites, electronic discussion groups, and other tools and resources to serve the NGO community were rapidly developed to continue this process of sharing information across boundaries. By the year 2000, many NGOs had a Web site or one under development. Most were also communicating extensively internally and externally by e-mail. These electronic communications opened up an extensive and easily accessible network of information about other NGOs and international trends that was available previously only through intensive research.

Impacts of Global Changes on Local Organizations

In the mid-1990s when these changes were first taking place, the impacts on the NGO community were initially thought to affect only larger NGOs, many of them already working internationally or plugged into a global network.

Over time, many locally based organizations began discovering that global awareness and thinking could strengthen their own programs and in some cases provide them with solutions or creative ideas to break through an obstacle or constraint they would have trouble working through otherwise. And increasingly they were discovering that they could find some model practices with real applicability locally in other countries.

Programs such as the United States Agency for International Development (USAID) Lessons Without Borders conferences, which started in 1994, began to help the dissemination of this information and encourage such exchanges. The USAID program focused on some of the back-to-basics, community-oriented approaches that have been successful in USAID's work overseas that could be applied to similar problems in the United States. But leaders of NGOs are largely in a position of trying to create their own networks and resources to find ways to deal with the increasingly international external environment they are facing.

Without fanfare, the staff and board leaders of locally based nonprofit organizations in the United States (and throughout the rest of the world) have used their own international contacts and perspectives to develop connections and programs to benefit the organizations they are involved with. As the chapters in this book lay out, their creative approaches have ranged from including international themes and speakers in their conferences and programs to integrating lessons or ideas from programs in other countries to their own organization's programs. Their colleague nonprofit leaders have much to learn from their efforts. With your reading of this book, your organization will be able to benefit from these experiences as well.

How This Book Is Organized

This book outlines a variety of approaches that organizations can take to enhance their international engagement. You may choose to read this book in its entirety or look for the sections that apply specifically to your organization's current situation. You may find that it will be helpful to keep this book close by and consult it regularly as your organization's international engagement evolves. This book is designed for nonprofit leaders and provides practical how-to advice. It outlines a variety of approaches an organization can take to enhance its international engagement.

Part One provides a general orientation to the concept of international engagement, why it can apply to even small or locally based organizations, and how to ensure that whatever steps you take to become more globally aware are compatible with your organization's mission and core goals, and thus sustainable over time. Part Two describes some initial programs an organization can develop as it begins to explore its growing interest in being more connected to the global community. Many of these ideas can be customized to your organization and accomplished with minimal financial resources. The chapters in this part address using your annual conference or other meetings as an international gateway, accessing international networks, developing strategic alliances and partnerships, and other programs that organizations have pioneered. Part Three looks at how an organization's operations can be modified (incrementally or in more significant ways if you are ready to do so) to make it a more actively engaged player in the international arena. The chapters address bringing international perspectives into your decision-making groups, expanding your international reach through membership, and communicating internationally, and it identifies some technical issues to be aware of as you venture forth internationally. Part Four describes some truly global organizations for the lessons that can be learned from the way they operate and some examples from countries outside the United States. Although this book focuses primarily on U.S. examples, Chapter Thirteen shows that the trend we see in the United States of going international is similar to those evolving around the rest of the world as well. Part Four may be especially helpful to readers outside the United States who may wonder if the suggestions and trends presented in this book are applicable in other parts of the world.

Finally, the Glossary and Bibliography will help you find your way through the sometimes confusing terminology used in the global NGO community and provide you with some additional resources.

Chicago, Illinois   Bonnie L. Koenig
December 2003

Acknowledgments

I would like to thank the following people for being so generous with their limited time in submitting language to strengthen the sections on their organizations: Victoria Ames, Karen Blaisdall, Katherine Campbell, John Crosby, Margery Daniels, Lori Gusdorf, Janet Koster, Michael Kenyon, Kimerly Rorschach, Charlie Rose, Isabel Carter Stewart, Eve Sullivan, and Kimberly Svevo.

Thank you to my colleagues and friends whose ongoing comments and support helped make this book a reality—Gayle Gifford, Hildy Gottlieb, and Maggie Hivnor—and to my editor, Dorothy Hearst, for her encouragement and always helpful comments.

Finally, I would like to thank my parents, Florence and Bruce Koenig, for their unwavering support in this and all my other projects, and my husband, Gerald Rosenberg, for being there with a sense of humor when I needed it most.

About the Author

Bonnie L. Koenig is a consultant who works with nonprofit organizations to develop their international programs and strategic thinking. Prior to beginning her consulting practice, Going International, she was the executive director of the nonprofit organizations Zonta International (with members in over sixty-five countries) and the Council of Great Lakes Governors. She has written and spoken widely on the subject of nonprofit organizations and international engagement and has lived in Australia, China, France, and Mauritania. She received her M.A. in international relations from Yale University.

Going Global for the Greater Good

Part One

Why Become More International?

How Your Organization Can Benefit

Chapter One

Finding Your Organization's Place in an Increasingly Global World

That the world is becoming more global has become a common phrase. So what does this increasing global interdependence mean to you as a nonprofit practitioner and to your organization? If you have been thinking that there is a place in the international arena for your nonprofit organization but you are not sure where or how to begin, this book is for you. If you have made some movement into the international arena but have not yet found the right niche for your organization, this book might help to stimulate some new thoughts. And if you already have experience in the sector, you might nevertheless benefit from the refresher course in this book.

When you and your organization make connections internationally, the work of your organization can have significant impacts internationally while helping your own organization and its local constituency at the same time. And it does not need to cost a lot.

Consider the case of the Chicago Foundation for Women (CFW), a successful community-based group that could have limited its focus locally but developed its international engagement and enhanced its local programs through the vision and experiences of its board members and staff. According to Isabel Carter Stewart, executive director of CFW in 2003,

> In 1995, on the occasion of the Fourth World Conference on Women in Beijing, the staff leadership of the Chicago Foundation for Women became mindful of the international context in which women's and girls' rights should be considered. The next logical step was to build on the Foundation's intention to create a broad based

community of women from across the patchwork quilt of cultures represented in the cosmopolitan arena of Chicago. Given the convening power of Chicago Foundation for Women, it was relatively easy to invite diverse women to the table to begin discussions that would seek common ground and lead to a local understanding—and embrace—of human security as the term relates to all women. Convening immigrant women from among our grantee partners and American women of all the backgrounds among our board and volunteers to discuss international issues that affect us locally allows us to be true to our mission and broaden the conversation at the same time."[1]

Volunteers of America (VOA) is another example of an organization that had a highly successful national program in the United States for over one hundred years and did not have to become more internationally engaged to continue to be successful. In fact, not all of its leadership was sure the organization should proceed in this direction when the idea was initially brought to its board by one of its members. But it did think the idea had enough potential for the continued success of the organization in a changing world that it decided to conduct a feasibility study on increasing its international engagement. Through this study, VOA determined that it would begin to develop an international program, but at a slow and deliberate pace. Five years later, it had successful networks and a joint venture with an overseas partner, all strengthening its national work.

Both of these organizations (and many more that you will read about in this book) have found that they could enhance their mission and improve their local and national programs by becoming more internationally engaged.

International engagement is a process of connecting with the international nonprofit community and the broader world around your organization in ways that can help to strengthen your local or national programs. Sometimes an organization will have its global awareness raised because an issue it is dealing with locally, such as environmental protection or controlling AIDS or other diseases, does not limit itself to geographical boundaries. The leadership of other organizations will decide to review global trends to see how their organization's work can benefit from what is happening in other parts of the world.

There are many ways to become strategically more internationally engaged, some of them quite simple and not as resource intensive as you may believe. From sharing ideas and lessons learned with nonprofit organizations in other parts of the world to inviting speakers to make presentations on topics of international interest, there are many ways to add an international dimension to your organization. This book offers ideas and practical tips from other organizations that can be put to direct use in your daily operations. You will also discover if going international is an interesting concept but not quite right for your organization—at least right now.

Often the leaders of local, regional, or national nonprofit organizations think that starting an international program is a significant undertaking to which they will need to allocate extensive resources. But as the information and organizational examples in this book demonstrate, you do not need to plunge in and form a full-scale international program right away.

Figure 1.1 shows a spectrum of increasing international involvement that many organizations travel along as they develop their international engagement. On the starting side of the spectrum (the left side of the figure) are organizations that are primarily locally or nationally based but are beginning to link their programs to international trends, or they have a few members from outside the United States. On the far right side of the spectrum are the organizations that are truly global, with members, programs, or operations in many different regions around the world and having a multinational board of directors or other decision-making group.

Figure 1.1. Spectrum of International Engagement

Local organization	Local organization with international awareness	Local organization with international programs	Organization with members or programs in different countries	Organization in alliance/ network	Global organization

We often think of organizations as being either local or global in nature. Although the focus is often placed on organizations at either end of the spectrum, many organizations lie at different stages along this spectrum of international engagement. It is important to realize that such a spectrum exists to know that there are many options and models that can be used as a guide in choosing the level of engagement best suited to your organization. Some organizations continue on a path along this spectrum toward a greater international engagement, and others find compatibility with their missions and programs at the beginning parts of the spectrum. They may broaden their international awareness but not change their core constituency or organizational structure.

Organizations along the spectrum vary by the degree of international engagement, as well as the type of international engagement they choose. As organizations move along the spectrum (toward the right side of the line), they are developing a greater degree of international engagement—for example, having more members from outside the United States, more programs with international partners, or more overseas partners or advisers involved in their programs, conferences, or decision making. Along the spectrum are different types of international engagement that an organization can choose. For example, as you will see in succeeding chapters, organizations can become more internationally engaged through their annual conference or other meetings (Chapter Four), through networking or partnership with organizations from other countries (Chapters Five and Six), or through their membership or decision-making structures (Chapters Eight and Nine).

For examples of organizations on the beginning side of the spectrum—those with international awareness and some international programs—you can read more about the Chicago Foundation for Women and the Association for Volunteer Administration in Chapter Four. For examples of organizations further along the spectrum, one that has chapters in a few countries and one that has a network of partners in many parts of the world, read about the Association of Fundraising Professionals and Sister Cities International in Chapter Nine. And for the truly global organization with activities or operations throughout the world and a multinational board of directors, take a look at Chapter Twelve, which is devoted to these organizations and the lessons that organizations at earlier stages of internationalization can learn from them.

The goal of this book is to demonstrate to organizations that are feeling this pull into the global arena and would like to have a greater engagement with an increasingly global world that there are many options. It is indeed possible to be connected to a global community and benefit from this network without changing your mission or dramatically altering existing programs or operations. This book also explores the trends of locally or nationally based organizations that are becoming more international and provides specific examples to illustrate these trends. Many of these projects have been previously undocumented as examples of the increasing international awareness of the nonprofit community and will be helpful to colleague nonprofit organization leaders looking for models and the experiences of others to learn from.

To be effective, international engagement needs to be customized to the organization. The many ideas provided in this book are intended to be illustrative, not prescriptive. There are many ideas that are presented for your organization to consider, refine, build on, modify, or otherwise adapt as appropriate to your goals and resources.

This book will help you to address some of the fundamental questions that are important to consider before embarking on a path of international engagement. Why does your organization want a greater international engagement? What are the opportunities? What obstacles might you face? How can you best prepare your organization to go down this path? Do you want to just follow international issues and trends, occasionally identifying some opportunities, or be actively involved in international activities? Do you want to import (be the receiver), export (be the giver), or facilitate (be a catalyst) the sharing of cross-border knowledge? The answers to these questions will affect the strategies you pursue to accomplish your goals.

Chapter Two

Expanding Your Global Outreach by Developing a Global Mind-Set

"Think globally but act locally" and newer variations, such as "Think globally *and* act globally," are nice expressions, but what do they really mean, and how does your organization put them into practice?

Because you are reading this book, you probably already have an interest in the world around you. Now the organizational questions become (1) What does your organization have to gain by being more globally aware? (2) How do you as a leader help bring this perspective into the organization's culture? and (3) How do you assess where on the spectrum of international engagement your organization currently is and where you would like to go?

It used to be that organizations operated either domestically or internationally, and these were mutually exclusive areas. Few organizations saw themselves as serving a constituency or existing in an environment that comfortably covered local, national, and international concepts. Much of these artificial distinctions have now become blurred, however, and strategic leaders see their organization, no matter how small or local, as part of a global community.

Becoming internationally aware does not just happen by itself, and it does not happen quickly. You can use your leadership position to begin this ongoing process within your organization. To bring about change in the organization's culture, you will need to build a commitment among the leadership and staff of your organization to a shared understanding and vision.

What's to Be Gained by Your Organization's Being More Aware of the World Around It?

Let's first look at the question of what is to be gained by your organization's being more aware of the world around you. You may already be convinced of some of these reasons but may find it useful to have some additional language to articulate it to others within your organization who are less sure:

- You will be open to discovering ideas from other cultures or countries that might be beneficial to your organization's own national or local programs.
- You will become more supportive and respectful of multicultural diversity among your organization's leadership, members, and staff members.
- Your local programs may become more effective with an improved understanding of and response to a diverse client group's key issues.
- You may expand your program's reach by more successfully reaching critical immigrant and ethnic target groups within the United States with your program services.
- You will increase your credibility with the growing group of members, clients, donors, and others who travel and think internationally.

Qualities of Those Who Are Internationally Aware

Much has been written about what makes a good global manager, with most of this material designed for the corporate sector (some of these books are listed in the Bibliography). Several of the characteristics that have been identified by those operating primarily in the private sector clearly apply to anyone in the corporate, governmental, or nongovernmental sectors who would like to be more internationally aware, seeking out opportunities that apply to their professional work.

They think in terms of the big picture and seek out world trends, looking at how they make global-local connections relevant in their own lives. They are open as well to new ideas and different ways of doing things, and they accept that intercultural interactions and relationships often involve ambiguity. In the United States, we often want a tangible answer (usually a simple yes or no) and then proceed from there. Many other cultures, however, are more complex in how they approach concepts and decision making; for example, sometimes there may be no clear yes or no answer. The internationally aware learn to work with such ambiguities, modifying their own thinking and processes rather than fighting against different cultural approaches.

Finally, those who are internationally aware are flexible. They rely on organizational processes rather than a set structure to deal with the unexpected. A dynamic process approach to decision making will allow those who are responsible for implementing your organization's goals in a complex and changing world to use their own judgments to respond to unexpected challenges. Those who are internationally aware are often more comfortable with the responsibility that comes with this type of process than those who have a more local perspective and feel that they need to follow a more formal structure that clearly specifies what they can or cannot do in any given situation. This characteristic certainly is not limited to those who are internationally aware, but those with an international awareness often have experience that strengthens their ability to be flexible.

You might want to be on the lookout for some of these characteristics in your volunteer leaders or staff. People who have cultivated these skills on their own can often provide helpful support in influencing your organization's perspectives.

How to Develop an Organization's Appreciation for International Thinking

Building the needed commitment to a shared vision of global awareness can start with some initial board and staff discussions of the advantages of moving in this direction.

After these discussions and initial commitment to these ideas, or if your organization already has some international members or an initial international program, or you have begun to move along the spectrum of international engagement, there are a number of ways to begin to integrate international thinking into the staff's daily operations to make them more effective:

- Survey the staff for their language capabilities. This will send the message that languages are important and will identify expertise that your organization has but may not be aware of. This is especially important if you currently have some international members or are interacting in other ways with members of the global community. Circulate the list of language capabilities within the organization among appropriate volunteer leaders and the staff so they are aware of this expertise and can tap it when needed.
- Distribute handouts that highlight cultural aspects that may affect your workplace or overseas members. This might include a listing of major religious holidays and national days observed by your members.
- Develop a list of tools that staff can use to better serve an international membership or communicate with others throughout the world they come in contact with. Include Web sites that have currency conversions, country telephone codes, country video standards, time zones, and other useful information.
- At a staff meeting, try some role playing designed to develop sensitivity to cultural differences in a variety of settings and situations. Those who may not be used to thinking about different cultural approaches to business situations may be uncomfortable with those from other cultures or countries or might offend someone without ever realizing that they have done so. Staff who become sensitized to cultural differences will become more aware of the research they may need to do before entering an international environment (such as a conference with international attendees) or at a minimum remember to choose their words more carefully.

For example, have one participant play an attendee from another country at your organization's annual meeting and another participant be a staff member who is handling the attendee's welcome at the registration area. Or have one participant play a visitor who comes to your office to find out about your organization's work but speaks very limited English, someone else play the receptionist who first encounters the person, and another participant the person whom the visitor will be directed to for more information.

• Have periodic staff sessions (perhaps as part of an informal bring-your-own lunch series) with invited outside guests to discuss international topics. A nearby consulate might provide a speaker, or nearby universities may have visiting scholars. Designate someone on your staff, or ask the speaker, to pay close attention to how the topics they are addressing apply to your organization's work.

• Look for ways to expose the staff to an international environment or varied perspectives as often as possible. For example, when an international visitor comes to the organization's office, have that person meet with as many staff members as possible at lunch or by walking them through the office to meet the staff informally. The experience can be enhanced be sending the entire staff information in advance about the visitor with a paragraph or two about his or her home country. Ask the guest to give a brief presentation about your organization's field of interest in his or her country, or if time does not permit a verbal presentation, circulate it in writing to the staff.

• Encourage interns from outside the United States to work with your organization, and plan to learn from them as they learn from you.

• Try a staff game focused on international topics such as "international trivia." You might have the winner receive something from another country brought back from the travels of a board member.

• Get involved on listservs (electronic discussion groups via e-mail) that have participants from organizations in other parts of the world. As access to the Internet grows and more people from around the world participate on these lists, these forums are increasingly providing a window to the (nongovernmental) world, with useful insights into different cultural approaches to issues that may be of interest to your organization.

- Attend conferences that have presentations on global issues in your field or international attendees. Be sure to take advantage of these opportunities to seek out the non-U.S. attendees you may have something in common with, or make a point of attending a panel with non-U.S. presenters. When volunteer leaders or staff members attend such a conference, ask them to share some of what they have learned with others in the organization. The more they can make the linkages between what they have learned and your organization's work and interests, the more useful this information exchange will be.

- Attend international discussions through the professional organizations you and your staff members may belong to, and determine what related organizations may be involved in international projects or networks. (See Chapter Five for more information on networking.)

What to Be Aware of When Operating in a Global Environment

As your organization begins to move along the spectrum of international engagement, there are some ongoing issues you should keep in mind.

Cross-cultural relationships take time to build. Many cultures are more formal than Americans are used to and want to establish a relationship before getting down to business. Make sure that your leadership and staff have realistic expectations about the time commitment involved. You will see with many of the examples in Chapter Six on partnerships that these partnerships took time to cultivate.

Americans often focus on what they have to teach the world. Send the message that you are interested in learning from other cultures as well, and be willing to listen at least as much as you speak.

Recognize that multiculturalism and multinationalism are different. Multiculturalism exists within one country. Although people have different cultural perspectives, these views are modified by receiving the same political messages, reading the same newspapers, and watching the same television programs. The context in which decisions are made is thus similar. In many cases, someone from another culture living in the United States has learned to modify his or her culture to suit local expectations. In multinationalism, this common context does not exist. Hence, cultural differences are more pronounced. Working on understanding different cultures will help you in both situations, but be aware that the lessons are not completely interchangeable. For example, someone from a country where the authority of senior managers is followed without question may realize that this is not the culture of your organization but nevertheless may not be comfortable with speaking out. In their own country, they may have developed methods with their colleague workers to deal with this when they have concerns, but by themselves in your organization, they may just keep quiet and any problems they have may neither be articulated nor dealt with.

Do not underestimate the role that culture plays for many people and how it may affect your organization. This may manifest itself in anything from individual contacts with someone from Asia who may not want to directly give you bad news or say something they believe is an answer you do not want to hear, to how your organization may need to develop policy if your decision making incorporates those from other cultures.

If your organization already has international members or connections, there are some practical steps you can take to modify the way you do business, from those that are easy to do to those that may be more time intensive but will demonstrate your organization's true commitment to being an international player. Be aware of the messages you are sending, and then modify any messages that may not be sending a positive message to those of other nationalities.

Some Easy Steps

Once your leadership and staff have begun to make a commitment to being more internationally aware and culturally sensitive, there are some small steps they can keep in mind during their ongoing interactions within an international environment. You may be surprised at how even the smallest of gestures will send a very positive signal:

- Minimize your use of acronyms and idiomatic expressions (including those you may consider to be in common usage— for example, "thinking out of the box") when speaking with a multinational group or non-U.S. individuals. Even those who are conversant in English may have difficulty understanding colloquialisms.

- Take time zones into consideration when scheduling conference calls with overseas participants. If the time chosen is less convenient for some participants, consider switching this for the next call so all participants can share in any inconvenience.

- Adjust your fill-in forms or membership database so that you can accommodate a country identification and non-U.S. addresses and telephone numbers.

- Be aware of the nonverbal messages you are sending, and make them internationally sensitive. For example, if you usually show the United States at the center of a map or globe, try versions that rotate the part of the world that is front and center.

- Add an international column or an international perspective to domestic stories in your publications.

- If you are a membership organization, consider having a new committee or task force chaired or cochaired by a non-U.S. member.

More Challenging Activities to Consider

Where is your organization on the spectrum of international engagement, and where would you like to move toward? If you have not yet had this discussion within your organization or have not had it in a while, review Chapter Three on integrating international perspectives into your strategic planning. If your organization is already aware of and committed to an increasing international engagement, you can implement this commitment by trying some of the ideas that follow.

When your organization is further along the spectrum of making a commitment to international awareness, try analyzing all of your programs and services through a global filter to determine how they are being perceived by non-U.S. members or other target groups. Initially, you might want to do this in a streamlined fashion by having a few staff members or volunteers look at some sample products and programs to identify what messages they believe are being sent. Do your registration forms accommodate various surnames, postal codes, and countries, for example? Or if a program has a goal that talks about enhanced media exposure but all of the success stories given are of U.S.-based media, what message might that be sending to non-U.S.-based members? Does a member who telephones your headquarters get a faster response than someone from another country who communicates by e-mail or fax? Going through such an exercise can be very illuminating to your staff and volunteers.

You can also initiate a complete international assessment or review. This might include sending a survey to non-U.S. members or advisers or having several task forces (including U.S. and non-U.S. members) review different products and services. (See the international assessment questions at the end of this chapter for more information.)

Also consider conducting a more formal training of your organization's board of directors and staff on internationalism. You can do this in-house or with a professional trainer. (A fuller discussion of board training is contained in Chapter Eight.) For staff training, if you are a larger organization, be sure to include staff members from throughout the organization rather than limiting this to those with the international or membership services portfolios. Providing this training opportunity to others throughout the organization will help to maximize your chances that new ideas will be success-fully implemented and send the message that this is not just a token process. An international orientation or program will be most effective if everyone shares an understanding of the organization's approach to internationalism and how its implementation may' involve various parts of the organization.

Many organizations find that they enter a process of interna-tional awareness and engagement by having members or other guests from overseas attend their annual meeting. If this is the case with your organization, consider devoting part of your initial meet-ing planning sessions to an orientation on making overseas atten-dees feel welcome and enhancing the international opportunities for all members at the meeting. Feature some non-U.S. guests as speakers, or host an international reception. (For additional ideas on making your meetings more international see Chapter Four.)

Increasing an organization's international perspectives is an ongoing process. Integrating this effort into a dynamic strategic planning process will recognize this need for continued commit-ment. For each part of your strategic plan, you may want to ask a number of questions. How does it reflect an international engage-ment with the world? How will it be viewed by the organization's membership and constituents, especially those from outside the United States or those especially committed to global perspectives? What messages will it send about the organization externally? (For additional information on integrating global perspectives into a strategic planning initiative, see Chapter Three.)

Ready to Start?

The key in initiating any new change is to know where you are headed and then to get started in a manageable way.

If you want your organization to become more aware of the world around you, have an initial staff discussion with some brief presentations, and follow up with some of the ideas in this chapter. If you like the idea of your organization's becoming more internationally oriented but need an internal discussion to see if the leadership shares this perspective, put a discussion on the agenda for your next meeting. If your organization is already committed in principle but you need to put some action and momentum behind these words, consider one international idea you can implement within the next thirty to sixty days and what you can put in an implementation plan over the next year.

Once you have started, remember to think about sustainability. Raising international awareness and cultural sensitivity is an ongoing process that will take the ongoing commitment of the entire leadership and staff.

International Assessment Questions

If your organization is considering expanding its international engagement, a good way to begin is by having your leadership address some of the following questions. After this initial discussion, if more information is needed, it can be gathered by a survey sent to non-U.S. members or target audience or by a more thorough internal analysis of your programs.

Motivation

- Whose idea is it to have your organization engage more internationally: the board, other volunteer leaders, the staff, or others?
- Who are the champions who are encouraging others to adopt these new perspectives? Why are they encouraging this?
- Are there skeptics? What are their concerns?

Organization Culture and Structure

- Is your organization's culture open to a broader outlook on the world?
- Are your mission and vision compatible with international engagement?

- If changes are needed, is your organization good at adapting to change?

Programs

- Do you already have international attendees at your meetings?
- Do you already have international subscribers to your publications?
- Do those from outside your home country use your other programs in any way?

Meetings

- Do your meetings offer programs of international interest?
- Are your meetings easy for overseas attendees to participate in?
- Are your programs accessible to potential international users?

Publications

- Do your publications have articles with themes of international interest?
- Do your publications have articles by international authors? Do you encourage your international colleagues to submit articles or your staff to solicit them?
- Do you minimize the use of slang or non-U.S.-specific acronyms or expressions?

Other Programs

- Are your other programs accessible to potential international users?

Membership

- Do you currently have international members? What percentage of your membership do they comprise?
- How are their expectations of membership similar to those of your domestic members? How are they different?

- Are there areas of the world where your current members are grouped or noticeably absent?
- Are your international members active?
- How are your international members represented in your organization?
- Can they (and do they) serve on committees and hold other leadership positions?
- Are there specific challenges associated with their involvement?
- Have you looked at the cost of membership to your international members in relation to the benefits they receive?

Chapter Three

Integrating Global Perspectives into Strategic Planning

For your organization's international initiatives to be most effective, they must advance its general mission, meet specific objectives and strategies, and be well integrated into the overall goals of the organization. If an international orientation does not flow logically from your organization's mission statement or strategic plan, it may be a mistake to force it.

To determine if your organization should pursue a greater international engagement, begin by asking a few fundamental questions, including an analysis of what your organization hopes to accomplish by becoming more engaged internationally. For example, does your organization want to provide greater value to members or constituents wherever they may reside in the world? Or can your organization's mission be furthered by a greater awareness of worldwide trends?

Beginning the Analysis

Here are some initial questions to ask about internationalism to help guide your review.

What Is Motivating the Organization's Interest in an Increased International Engagement?

It will be important to determine if this interest is compatible with your organization's mission statement and objectives. Although it may take you in some new directions, these directions should be building from your overall foundation. For example, when Volunteers of America decided to explore a greater international engagement, its leadership determined that its mission of providing local human service programs and opportunities for individual and community involvement was increasingly relevant worldwide. Other organizations conducting a similar analysis have determined that their work would continue to be most effective in their local area and that to develop a greater international engagement would divert resources away from this work, not enhance it.

It may take some organizational discipline to resist the lure of the notion of international involvement and focus on whether a greater international engagement truly is compatible with and enhances the organization's mission. If it does not fit comfortably, do not force it.

How Will Increased Attention to International Trends Advance the Organization's Mission?

Once you have determined that an increased international engagement is compatible with your organization's mission, the next step is to identify how it will help to forward the organization's mission as any use of your resources should do. Determine whether an increased international orientation or international program will strengthen your service to members or your constituent group (or groups). Be sure as well to develop your reasoning to convince skeptics that this is indeed a good use of the organization's resources.

What Is Your Vision for the Future? What Role Will International Activities Play in Your Organization's Overall Vision for Itself?

When your organization is involved in strategic planning, it will be looking at its vision for several years in the future. As part of this exercise, this is a good time for your organization to look at the place it sees for itself along the spectrum of international engagement (see

Figure 1.1). Where are you now on the spectrum, and where would you like to move?

Use the questions in the international assessment at the end of Chapter Two (and others you may develop) to help you assess where you are on the international engagement spectrum. This is not always an easy exercise. Some boards of directors are split on what point of the spectrum they are starting at and where they would like to go. You should also include a cost-benefit analysis that identifies the benefits you hope to derive in relation to your anticipated costs.

Once you reach a decision, make sure that you articulate the international aspects of the vision you have chosen. When the International Association of Jazz Education (IAJE) created its future vision in 2000, its leadership felt that the organization should integrate its growing international membership and over time become a truly global organization (the right-hand side of the spectrum in Figure 1.1).

As a result of this discussion, your organization may decide that it does not see itself being proactively engaged internationally or want an international program as part of its overall vision for itself, or that it would like the international engagement to stay small within a clearly U.S.-oriented organization. These are options that should be considered as well. The commitment needed to sustain international engagement is significant, and if that commitment is not there, you might be best served by deciding this now before proceeding further down this road.

What Does the Organization Hope to Accomplish Through Internationalism?

Once you have decided that pursuing a greater international engagement is compatible with your organization's mission and may help to forward it, identify the specific goals you hope to accomplish by exploring this area further. They might include increasing your organization's knowledge base, sharing your organization's expertise more widely, or supporting non-U.S. members more effectively. Other ideas can be found in the succeeding chapters. As with any other effective strategic planning process, the strategies you develop to meet these goals should be determined by the goals you identify.

How Quickly Should Your Organization Move Ahead?

The answer to this question depends on some of the time frames you have developed for other parts of your strategic plan and the organizational resources available. In all cases, make sure to look at the sustainability of the international engagement or program you are developing. Having a well-developed plan will allow you to determine how fast you can proceed. If there are insufficient resources or concerns within the organization's leadership or members regarding this new direction, you may decide to proceed more cautiously, with clear markers for success along the way. As you reach each target goal, you can analyze what you have learned and determine if and how you should proceed. Reviewing your progress at clearly defined stages will help you to change directions or even eliminate this program if it is not continuing to serve the organization's mission.

Elements to Help You Review Your Progress

- Set target (benchmark) goals initially.
- Define what your measures of success should be.
- Define the assessment process and timetables.
- Periodically review progress.
- Revise strategy, goals, and measures as needed.

Making and Communicating the Decision

The most effective actions will be chosen based on your organization's own mission and goals. Ideally, this analysis of the organization's international goals should be done as part of an overall strategic planning initiative. And as with general strategic planning, the most effective internationalization process will be customized to the organization. What works well for one organization may not work equally well for another. However, there are steps that have been taken by organizations that have successfully made this journey that can be helpful to others. Two models and some example organizations are examined later in this chapter.

Once you have gone through the initial analysis, determined what you hope to accomplish, and made a decision to proceed, the reasoning behind this decision should be communicated to your organization's members, staff, and other stakeholders. The further along the global spectrum you have decided to move, the more important it will be to vest your members, staff, and other constituent groups in this vision for the organization. Developing the international relationships that may be part of achieving your international goals will take time and money, and the entire organization must feel that this commitment is worthwhile, and important.

An international program will be most effective if all parts of the organization share an understanding of the organization's approach to internationalism and how its implementation may involve various parts of the organization. For example, if your organization determines that it wants to make its operations more sensitive to its non-U.S. members or constituents, the publications department will need to integrate this orientation into its publications just as much as the membership division does (see Chapter Eight). If international perspectives are integrated throughout the organization's operations, the leadership will be able to act strategically based on globally oriented information that is forwarded to it by committees, staff, and other organizational groups. Otherwise, it may be left to deal with filling in the gaps and dealing with any difficulties that develop when it does not receive full information to structure its decision making.

Vesting your organization's stakeholders in this process will be critical to its success. You may want to create a checklist of stakeholders to refer to throughout the process: in its initiation, as the plan is being developed, as information is being obtained, as challenges are being faced, and in all of your communications about the planning process. Such a checklist will vary from one organization to another, but it may include the following:

- All members of the leadership: the board of directors, executive committee, committee chairs, and others.
- All staff.
- Members (if you are a membership organization), clients (to whom you provide services), and other constituent groups (you may represent).
- International members, constituents, or advisers, especially if you are at the early stages of having international members or developing an international perspective. The ideas of those from outside the United States will be critical to your U.S. members. And it will be important to any continuing international enhancement you hope to undertake for non-U.S. members or other stakeholders to feel included.
- Donors, especially those who may be particular supporters of or skeptics about international engagement.
- Partner organizations.

The sensitivity and awareness to the way an organization's constituents or members anywhere in the world will respond to its programs from an international or multinational perspective is something that both membership and nonmembership nonprofits should focus on. In order to gain and retain non-U.S. members, membership organizations should understand how these members view each of the organization's programs as responding to their interests and needs. In a nonmembership organization, the need also exists to gain and retain constituents who support the organization's mission from a financial (donor) perspective or to give the organization programmatic legitimacy. For an organization's international program or orientation to be successful, it must be made evident to these constituents how this focus on international engagement will advance the mission and goals of the organization.

Exploring Increased International Engagement

There are two primary ways that organizations generally explore their understanding of and commitment to increasing their international engagement: forming a committee to explore possible international initiatives or integrating globalization goals into the organization's general goals and strategic plan.

International Committee Model

If a committee is leading the effort, its members can integrate the program into the organization and give it its best chance for success in several ways:

- Involving the organization's leadership outside the international committee structure, such as board members and committee chairs, in the international strategy development sessions
- Surveying organization leaders about their goals for the international program and their perceptions of the challenges of developing such a program
- Keeping organizational leaders and members informed of new international strategies that are developed and actions that are taken
- Asking the organization's leaders to outline why the association is pursuing an international program and how it will accomplish it
- Asking the organization's leaders to play a lead role in working with their peers who may be less comfortable with moving in this direction

To respond to an increasing interest and involvement among its member physicians in international issues, the American Osteopathic Association (AOA) created a committee to explore possible international initiatives. Over several years, the work of the committee helped to build a constituency for an international program beyond the small group who had originally advocated an AOA role in this area. Initially, committee members worked independently, developing a separate strategic plan. After several years of publicizing and implementing its goals and activities, including a successful international seminar at the association's annual conference, the committee's work naturally integrated into the association's strategic plan and became an integral part of the association's long-term vision.

Integration Within the Strategic Plan Model

Most effective strategic planning addresses the question of what resources will be needed to implement each proposed program: financial, human resources, and others. (See the Bibliography for sources on strategic planning.) When an organization is looking to integrate international programs or perspectives, a global filter can be used in the same way as this resource filter. For each part of the proposed strategic plan, consider how it will reflect an international engagement with the world, how it will be viewed by the organization's membership and constituents (especially those from outside the United States or those especially committed to global perspectives), and what messages it will send about the organization externally. If an international orientation is tacked on as a stand-alone program, its life may be short and ineffective.

Increasing an organization's international perspectives must be seen as an ongoing process. Integrating this effort into a dynamic strategic planning process will recognize this need for continued organizational commitment. Integrating international perspectives throughout an organization's programs and activities is a long-term commitment of leadership investment, time, and resources.

The wording chosen to discuss this issue can be important in helping to clarify the leadership's thinking regarding where along the global spectrum it wants the organization to be. A discussion of whether your organization is developing a "strategic plan with a global perspective" or a "global strategic plan," for example, may help to clarify this thinking. Developing and implementing a truly global strategic plan will need to include a change of mindset—one that moves away from focusing more on the domestic part of the organization toward making a commitment that everything the organization produces will reflect an international perspective.

In order to carry a global filter through the strategic planning process, some organizations include an international specialist or non-U.S. member on each task force that is part of its strategic planning process. An alternative is to have an international specialist or non-U.S. member review each proposed part of the plan.

To make the transition from international as a separate program to internationalism as core to the organization, the benefits of integrating international perspectives throughout the organization should be modeled in the planning process. Thus, all committees should reflect an international perspective and involve U.S. and non-U.S. participants.

When the International Association of Jazz Education (IAJE) initiated a strategic planning process, it integrated an existing international committee into its overall strategic planning process and incorporated an international component into each of the strategic directions it identified. Each strategic planning process task force included at least one non-U.S. member. The IAJE already had active non-U.S. chapters and representatives on its board, and its situation was primed for integration. Nevertheless, it still took a committed leadership to move in this direction.

Here are some additional ways to integrate international perspectives within the strategic planning process:

- For each step of the strategic planning process and section of the plan, ask how an international program might advance the organization's mission and goals. You will want to know that this international orientation will support as many parts of the organization and its programs as possible.

- In order for an increased international orientation to be understood as compatible with the organization's overall mission and goals, it will be important to clarify and clearly articulate what your organization hopes to accomplish with this international engagement.

- Have a non-U.S. member or key constituent cochair the strategic planning task force, and include non-U.S. members or constituents on all of the strategic planning committees. This will model a commitment to learning from other parts of the world and send a clear message to non-U.S. members or constituents that other perspectives are indeed important.

- If your organization has a preexisting international committee, include it early on in the strategic planning process. If your goal is to integrate international perspectives into your strategic planning process, an existing international committee that has already been dealing with international perspectives and issues may help others to broaden their horizons. They can be spokespeople for how your international goals can enhance the organization overall.

- Ensure that all of the organization's stakeholders are vested in the commitment to integrating international perspectives within the strategic planning process. This will take an ongoing commitment of your organization's leadership and staff. You will increase your chances for succeeding in this task by involving key stakeholders in this process from the very beginning. The more they understand the value of including international perspectives in their work, the greater the commitment to doing so will be. Ultimately, for changes to be successful, the leadership and staff need to be engaged.

Tapping into their experiences and creativity will help everyone who is crucial for taking this forward to feel part of the process.

Communicating the Importance of International Perspectives

Those charged with incorporating international thinking into the overall planning process need to share a vision of why internationalization is important to the organization's mission. The leadership that is championing the international integration process is important. A leader who is generally respected throughout the organization for his or her credibility on a wide range of issues will often be seen as more credible on the need for international integration than a leader who has made his or her organizational reputation on international issues.

The leadership will need to send consistent messages regarding the organization's commitment to integrating international perspectives to members or constituents. All stakeholders should understand the value of including the perspectives of those from outside the United States and how the entire organization will become stronger as a result. For some organizations, this may entail making a transition from a zero-sum mentality (with winners and losers) to a win-win one where everyone benefits. For others, it may be an understanding of why some short-term investment of resources will bring about some longer-term gains.

The organization's leadership should work to ensure that its language about becoming more international is followed by action. There are numerous organizations that use this language with the best of intentions or even add *international* to their name but never make the needed operational changes to become a truly international organization.

An important initial message to consider communicating is that the organization will be looking to ensure value for all members or constituents in the organization's program, regardless of where those members or constituents may reside in the world. (These programs and services may not be the same for all areas of the world, but there will be some parity in the value derived from them.)

The leadership will also want to understand and continue to remind others in the organization that internationalizing is an evolving process. Reasonable expectations of progress should be determined.

It could begin by conducting a survey of all members or constituent groups regarding ways in which they would like to receive value from their involvement with the organization and how they would like to see international perspectives incorporated. An assessment of the organization's program by staff, volunteers, or an independent consultant can determine how international the organization already is (see Chapter Two). Another step is to develop a leadership training program that will include cultural sensitivity training so that the organization's leaders can individually coordinate their verbal and nonverbal messages.

The Time Frame

International expansion can progress at a deliberate and fairly rapid pace, or it can be an evolving commitment over several years. Much of the timing will depend on the organization's culture and how ready it is to move in this direction.

The organizations mentioned in this chapter all took a different path and time frame based on their own situations. The IAJE already had active non-U.S. chapters and representatives on its board, and full integration was a natural next step. The AOA gradually evolved a constituency for these issues among its members. When the Volunteers of America (VOA) board began to discuss how the organization's programs could be enriched by a larger international engagement, their first step was to conduct a study of possible international opportunities. The VOA decided to proceed slowly so the program could be well integrated into its overall programs. Its first stage was to begin more extensive networking with sister organizations that had international programs.

Moving Forward

If your organization is initiating or is involved in an ongoing strategic planning process and you are also looking at how it might be more internationally engaged, be sure to integrate these two processes. An international plan that is not integrated into the organization's general strategic plan will not have the commitment needed to implement it and will not be sustainable over time. The ideas outlined in this chapter will provide some guidance as you create your own process so the results are sustainable.

The following checklist can serve as a reminder of the process outlined in this chapter:

_____ Analyze why your organization is contemplating a greater international engagement.

_____ Determine whether a greater international engagement is compatible with your mission.

_____ Identify what you hope to accomplish with a greater international engagement. (The strategy and tools you will want to develop will vary depending on the goals you commit to.)

_____ Establish a time frame for how quickly will you move ahead with your international engagement.

_____ Devise your international engagement plan, and determine whether it is integrated into your organization's overall strategic plan.

Part Two

The Initial Stages of International Program Development

Chapter Four

Using Your Annual Conference and Meetings as an International Gateway

If your organization is interested in expanding your engagement with the rest of the world, the annual conference can be a good place to start. You can help to expose your members and other attendees to international issues and themes in your field, often with minimal expense, by (1) better integrating those who currently attend your meeting from outside the United States and (2) encouraging attendance by colleagues from other countries or inviting speakers from other countries or those who are based in the United States and have expertise on international topics.

There are several options to consider to give your conference a broader international perspective. One way is to identify meeting topics that reflect globally oriented themes. You can include speakers or presenters from outside or from within the United States who have an expertise in internationally oriented issues. Begin by having international issues as one area that the program committee considers when identifying potential speakers or workshop topics. Identify what your organization would like to learn or accomplish, and generate topics accordingly.

You may want to target particular countries for attracting attendees. These may be locations where you already have some members or key contacts or you think your subject areas will be of particular interest. Targeting specific locations may also enable you to do some translations of publicity materials into the languages used in that location to make them more accessible to those you are trying to attract to your meeting. Highlighting the international aspects of the program in publicity materials will also help to interest potential attendees from outside the United States.

You can develop some special programs or courtesies for international attendees. Some organizations have an international reception or workshop and send special invitations to guests from outside the United States while inviting all members to attend. The networking opportunities benefit all who attend.

If space permits, you might consider an international lounge, where those interested in international networking can congregate. Some organizations have developed a fellows program, where members of the organization are assigned to first-time overseas attendees to help orient them to your conference. Especially for larger conferences, these gatherings can be intimidating to someone who is not familiar with the conference's format or is not a native English speaker.

Orient your program committee to some of the special courtesies (many of them easy to implement) that can help international attendees feel welcome and will encourage them to return again or develop a closer relationship with your organization. Examples are asking speakers to prepare handouts that will help those whose native language is not English to follow presentations more easily, or asking attendees on the registration form how they would like their name to read on their name badge so that it is in a format comfortable to their own cultural norms. Many other cultures prefer titles or full names to a nickname on a name badge or in a program.

Program Planning

You can maximize the benefits of incorporating globally oriented themes into your meeting by having those responsible for developing the conference program identify topics that reflect globally oriented themes of interest to members or regular conference attendees early in the planning process.

The Association for Volunteer Administration (AVA) added international topics and presenters to its annual conference as an easy way to begin addressing issues being raised by the increase of non-U.S. members and their impact on the organization and the profession. The board and staff realized the need for and benefits of tapping expertise in the profession from beyond North America. They identified incorporating more internationalism into the annual conference as a viable strategy for continuing to educate the majority of AVA members, who were Americans, to the fact that the organization supported and promoted a profession that is international. International topics can be submitted through the organization's request-for-proposal process or sought out or suggested by staff or board members who are aware of good presenters or topics.

Be sure to draw on the expertise of your leadership, members, and staff to identify timely topics and potential presenters. Consider sending out a questionnaire as a lead-up to the meeting planning to generate ideas. Or you might allocate some time at a board meeting to focus the board's attention on how their international knowledge and experiences outside the organization might be useful to other members of the organization.

The Chicago Foundation for Women, a local group, has been successful at integrating topics on global human rights, economic security, and political participation into the needs of its Chicago constituency, who out of "their own varied immigrant and U.S. national backgrounds, want their voices heard in the interest of making a difference on the global stage as well as in our city."[1] Much of the initiative for integrating these issues into the foundation's program came from the experiences of its board members and staff.

The Planning Process

When you hold a U.S.-based meeting with international attendees, you can increase the chances of having this be a positive experience for these individuals by keeping in mind some special considerations at each step of the planning process.

Preparing the Program

Spend some time in planning meetings going over the unique aspects of an international meeting, and give special attention to the cultural backgrounds of any large group of attendees from a particular country. For example, "saving face" with problems is important in some countries (particularly in Asia), and thus you may want to be especially sensitive to handling some issues quietly with these guests. For example, you may want to have someone available at registration who understands the preferences that Asian guests (especially speakers and other VIPs) may have of having any problems that may arise with their registration resolved quietly and not in front of all of the other who are registering at the same time.

Other unique aspects of an international meeting you may want to discuss initially with the planning committee include having a program that will appeal to a multinational audience, having an idea of the language capabilities of attendees, briefing of speakers to maximize their effectiveness in speaking in front of an international audience, and special audiovisual needs that may arise (such as making sure that the equipment is compatible with items that speakers may bring for audience viewing).

Marketing Materials and Publicity

All materials that go outside the United States should include the country name in the mailing address and provide the U.S. national telephone code (which is 1). Remember that toll-free telephone numbers are generally accessible only from within the United States, so if you are providing a toll-free number for American registrants, also provide a direct-dial number for those outside the United States.

The prices given in registration materials should be labeled specifically as U.S. dollar prices because many other countries around the world also use "dollar" to denote their currency (Canada, Australia, and New Zealand are some of them). If hotel information and prices are provided, specifically indicate what that price includes or does not include. What about local taxes, for example, and meals? Consider other financial issues as well. How will attendees pay their registration costs? Will foreign checks, electronic transfers, or credit cards be accepted? Be as specific as possible as to the options available.

Research the most commonly used means of publicizing a meeting in the geographical areas you will be mailing to. Although e-mail has become more accessible around the world, it may not be the method that will generate the most responses. If you do use nonelectronic means of sending materials, remember to factor in the time mail takes to reach different locations so potential attendees have adequate time to respond. Attendees from some countries may need customized letters of invitation to process their visa into the United States and adequate time to process their documentation.

Meeting Orientation Materials

Special information should be provided for overseas visitors on such matters as typical cab fares, local travel times to the convention site for those who may not be housed in the convention hotel, rush hour information, tipping and other local protocol, and average monthly temperatures (with temperatures in Celsius as well as Fahrenheit). You may also give some dress suggestions—for example, how formal the sessions will be and whether attendees should bring a jacket or sweater for inside the meeting location during summer months. (This is important to note because buildings in many other parts of the world are not air-conditioned to the degree that they are in the United States, and overseas attendees may find themselves prepared for outside temperatures but not inside ones.)

If a significant number of attendees are coming from one country or region, ask the local planning committee about the cultural issues that you should be aware of. Ask cultural questions that you believe may specifically be an issue at the meeting. For example, you could include a question about dietary restrictions as attendees register or inquire of a member or attendee from that country or region as to what type of menu choices may or may not be appropriate. (Some organizations now include a vegetarian option in their menu choices.)

Communicating with Non-American Attendees

Small efforts at speaking another's language (even with poor pronunciation) are usually appreciated. Although English has become an international business language, this does not mean that everyone attending an overseas meeting will be as comfortable with it as native speakers are. Remember to speak slowly and enunciate clearly with those for whom English is not a native language (although remember that you are speaking to an adult, not a child), and avoid using acronyms and slang.

Many cultures are more formal than is common in the United States. It is thus often advisable to remain formal in your initial contacts with non-Americans so you do not risk offense. You may also want to be clear in your registration materials in asking how attendees would like to be listed in an attendees list, on their name badge, or in any other printed materials.

If you will be providing interpretation, determine the languages that are needed (you may be able to determine this through a question on your registration form), how many sessions will require interpretation, and the interpretation equipment that will be needed. Do not forget to include interpretation expenses in your meeting budget.

Handouts and Other Preparations for Speakers

Request that presenters submit their talk outlines and handouts before the meeting so they can be distributed prior to or during the session. It is often easier to follow the written word than the spoken one. Having this material in advance will be especially important if you will be using interpreters.

Provide the presenters with some guidelines for speaking to the audience they will be addressing. This should include as much information as you have about the specific audience, including the countries represented, their cultural backgrounds, and their language capabilities. The general tips you can provide on addressing a multinational audience include speaking slowly, minimizing the use of acronyms and colloquial expressions, summarizing, using visuals, and being open to differing perspectives during the question-and-answer period. (See Chapter Ten for more information on speaking to a multinational audience.) This type of information is especially important for speakers who may not be accustomed to multinational audiences, but it can also be a helpful reminder to veterans.

On-Site Logistics

Determine if any translation or interpretation facilities will be provided. (Note that *translation* is written, and *interpretation* is oral.) Smaller organizations especially may want to determine the number of participants needed to use this service to justify the cost. Alternatively, your organization may decide that offering this service is important for projecting an international image or cultivating relationships with those from a certain region of the world, and the costs should be absorbed. If you do provide simultaneous interpretation, familiarize your interpreters in advance with any special terminology of your field, and ensure that they speak a dialect that is appropriate to those they will be addressing. Providing background materials to the interpreters is also helpful.

There are other ways as well to make your guests comfortable and integrate them into the conference activities. Another idea to consider is to have key directional signs to different conference events written in the most popular languages of attendees or having host volunteers or other attendees who are bilingual wear identification markers (for example, a pin that says, *"Je parle français"*).

Also consider adding the home country and possibly the native language to the name badges of all participants. This information can help communication and networking among attendees.

Consider offering foreign currency exchange as part of your conference services, or provide information on where this service can be conveniently obtained. The location of Automatic Teller Machines (ATMs) that accept internationally networked cards might also be helpful to attendees who have these type of accounts.

The preferences of overseas visitors may be different from those from the United States in a way that will affect what you need to prepare for. For example, consider what the beverage of choice may be for any sessions providing refreshments depending on the countries of origin of the participants (mineral water or water without ice may be significantly more popular than flavored sodas with ice, for example).

If you will have speakers from overseas, find out in advance what their technical needs are. For example, multisystem audio-visual equipment may be needed if overseas speakers will be bringing videos, DVDs, or other materials to show because of the different systems used around the world.

Depending on the number of attendees from overseas and your resources, consider a welcome at the airport, a special registration line, or other considerations. These courtesies can be highly welcome.

Holding Meetings Overseas

An organization's leadership may want to consider holding a meeting outside the United States. This step should be taken only after careful review of the reason for doing so and the specific considerations that will need to be addressed for this meeting to be successful.

The Evaluation Process

If you are thinking about developing a program outside the United States at a particular location, you need to ensure that the program is a viable one there. An important asset will be a local sponsor or planning committee that will be your liaison to government officials, vendors, speakers, and others you will need to work with locally to ensure a successful meeting. This group will also provide you information about local customs, protocols, and holidays and may serve as a intermediary if translation is needed.

If this is your organization's initial meeting outside the United States, you may want to choose a location that is English speaking and has similar customs, such as Canada or the United Kingdom.

The location should be one that will forward your mission for holding the meeting outside the United States. Are you looking to expand your membership in a particular region? Do you know that your organization has potential for additional membership or a successful ongoing program in a region and would you like to help initiate this activity? If your organization is planning on developing a relationship with a sister organization in another country, a face-to-face meeting can be invaluable in establishing this relationship.

Outlining the rationale for taking your meeting overseas and clarifying your goals in doing so is a very important initial step. Although a meeting can be successful if the initial reason is that the organization has been invited by a local member, board member, or partner group, this alone is often not enough to ensure the meeting's success.

After going through this evaluation process, if your leadership decides it would not be cost-effective to hold a meeting outside the United States, you may be able to accomplish some of your goals, such as a more direct interaction with overseas colleagues, by considering a teleconference or videoconference instead. With a well-defined agenda, the timing of such a conference (and the costs associated with it) can be controlled. Teleconferences that include participants from a number of countries can be scheduled through telephone services that specialize in these type of calls.

Many cities have vendors that rent facilities for videoconferences. The cost of a videoconference may seem expensive, but it will seem more reasonable when it is compared to the cost of the same participants traveling to a meeting. Be aware, however, that not all countries have videoconferencing technology available, that if they do have it, it may not be reliable, and that the costs may be significant. The countries where your participants are located will thus be an important factor in considering a video-conference. If you do schedule a teleconference or videoconference with participants from overseas for the first time, do not forget to consider the differences in time zones.

Program Elements

It is especially important to the success of an overseas meeting for your organization to outline clearly what you plan to do and how you plan to do it. This level of detail will help to facilitate the communications between headquarters in the United States and the local host committee or other local contacts. The more specific you can be, the more you will minimize the chances for miscommunication to occur, and when problems do occur, you can help to resolve them by referring back to your initial plans and agreements.

Advance Planning

Although issues will come up that you could not have planned for, the more you consider the unique aspects of an overseas meeting initially, the more you can minimize last-minute surprises.

Although it may be obvious that a larger meeting (such as a conference for several thousand attendees) will entail more of this advance planning, do not underestimate the planning that will be needed for even a small group that will be meeting in another country.

Entry Requirements. Get information on the requirements for the country you will be visiting. Will all of those who are key to your meeting's success be able to obtain a visa if one is needed?

Capabilities of the Meeting City and Venue. Are there unique characteristics of the proposed city that may or may not work well for your organization? What are transportation options from the hotel and between locations within the city? For larger conferences, are there enough flights within a twenty-four- to forty-eight-hour time span for arriving and departing attendees? If it is a non-English-speaking country, how easy will be it for English-speaking members of your organization to find English speakers to help them?

In many countries, most hotels are smaller than those in the United States. Are there hotels that can meet your group's preferences for accommodations as well as the functions you are planning? For larger meetings, you may need to consider a convention center for meeting sessions if there is not adequate room in the available hotels.

For contracts, it is advisable to retain a lawyer who has experience with international contracts. (See Chapter Eleven for more information on hotel contracts.)

Financial Issues. What is the exchange rate for the U.S. dollar in the country you will be visiting? How much will your U.S. dollar buy? You may want to budget in a cushion for any exchange rate changes that take place from the time you begin planning your meeting to the time you hold it, or lock in a rate if possible. You can often minimize exchange fees by researching how international funds can best be received, used to pay bills in the host country, and transferred home. Your local bank, if it has international operations, may be able to advise you regarding these issues. Is there a value-added tax (VAT) you will need to plan for? (Many European countries have them.)

Shipping Regulations and Customs. If you will be shipping materials or goods to the meeting site or back to your home base, make sure to find out what export or import regulations may affect these shipments.

Local Customs. When you choose a tentative meeting date, check for local national holidays and religious observances. What are the usual summer vacation periods (in Europe, for example, summer vacations tend to be longer than those in the United States), and how long do they tend to be? If you are inviting local government officials or dignitaries, what protocols should you be aware of? What are the local customs for meal functions? For example, in some countries, eating a box lunch or conducting a business session through lunch is not a common practice. This is an area where a local representative who can serve as your liaison will be critical to ensuring that you avoid significant mistakes.

Orienting Attendees. If your attendees have traveled overseas previously, you will not need to prepare them for the generally smaller size of hotel rooms abroad and the need to be careful of water and certain foods in some countries. Even the most seasoned traveler, however, appreciates a reminder about conversions to temperatures in the Celsius system from Fahrenheit and what the current currency exchange rate is with the U.S. dollar. You may want to create a fact sheet with this basic information for your attendees.

Reminders for Planning Meetings

- Be clear about what you want your meeting to accomplish regarding international goals.

- Incorporate your international goals into your meeting planning from the very beginning.

- Decide what special considerations you will provide for international guests.

- Create a checklist with items to incorporate or remember.

- For meetings outside the United States, identify a local adviser, liaison, or host committee.

Chapter Five

Networking to Discover What Other Organizations Are Out There

One of the approaches that can make becoming internationally engaged more accessible to smaller or midsized organizations is to begin this process in a very manageable, incremental way. Each step that you take will provide you with further information as to whether your organization wants to continue along the path of increased international engagement and what the benefits and potential challenges might be.

A good way to begin your outreach is to work through the networks your organization knows best. Approach your task initially as you might a more locally based networking effort. You might call it "seeking information or recommendations" or "bringing people and organizations with mutual interests together," and start with those people or organizations you know best. Networking at the international level may seem a little more challenging, but the concepts are the same: start close to home, and work outward.

Networking and exchanging information with colleagues from other countries may provide an additional benefit to your members or constituents by increasing the information available to them in their own professional work. It can strengthen your organization's own local programs and in some cases provide solutions or creative ideas or models that can be customized to your own programs. Finally, it can increase your ability to move a transnational agenda forward that may have local impacts, such as environmental protection or public health maintenance. In many countries, networking, identifying potential local partners, and building relationships may also be the key to accomplishing your specific goals. For example, understanding the system and the right people to speak with may be the only way to gain approval for the exchange of certain information, cultural exchange of colleague professionals, or holding a seminar. Having the local partners explain the system to you and make the necessary contacts may be the only way (and certainly the quickest way) to organize these programs. Using your existing networks and being referred to people in other countries by someone closer to home you already work with or trust will help you to identify the people overseas to work with and whom you can trust. Identifying potential partners is often not an easy task, and it can be complicated by cultural and often language barriers. Having the benefit of local introductions can be invaluable.

How to Approach Networking at the Global Level?

Keep in mind that the basic concepts of networking are the same at the global level as locally: you are looking to identify people or organizations that your organization has something in common with and that you would like to get to know better.

The best place to start is with your existing networks. (You may find the Web sites listed in the Bibliography useful too.) Survey staff and board members regarding professional societies or other organizations they belong to that may have an international component. Discuss with your local sister organizations networks they may have that extend internationally. You will probably discover all types of connections and resources that you had not known existed.

In your day-to-day activities, begin to look for items of interest that may have an international connection:

- Have any board members or staff traveled recently and learned information of professional interest? Ask them to share this information with the organization.
- Has anyone seen an interesting reference to an international theme or non-U.S. organization in a newspaper or magazine?

- Does a meeting or conference you are attending have any internationally oriented speakers or sessions?

The more you keep your eyes open and talk about your international interests, the more information you will identify or the more you will be approached by others with similar interests. Remind board members and staff to share these personal experiences with the organization.

Be creative about exploring new outlets. Perhaps there are forums for the discussion of internationally related issues in your local area that you have never paid much attention to because you believed they were irrelevant to your organization's work. Once you start attending some of these sessions or reading internationally oriented publications, you may discover there are more relevant ideas around the globe than you realized. Some of the examples provided in this chapter demonstrate how even very small, locally based organizations have benefited from international outreach. Be willing to minimize the often artificial barrier between what is often perceived as domestic and what is considered to be foreign or international.

Be open to a range of options as well, from the one-time exchange of information to an ongoing relationship. Do not prejudge a relationship until it has a chance to develop. As you get to know other organizations and the work they do better, you will be able to clarify each other's expectations, and the options for cooperation will become clearer. Your initial outreach does not always need to lead to your organization's becoming involved in a formal ongoing relationship with international partners. Although that may be one option, there are many others to consider that may be more informal or time limited, making them more manageable to your organization's own goals and resources.

Once you have identified specific goals regarding a potential new relationship, make sure you clarify these goals and expectations within your organization and then with your potential partners. Are you looking just to exchange information, or are you open to a more formal cooperative effort? What resources is your organization willing to allocate to this effort? Clarifying these goals and articulating them at the early stages of a relationship can help to avoid complications at later stages.

Be prepared to invest the time to cultivate these relationships. In many cultures, taking the time to build a personal relationship is a necessity before any professional cooperation can be considered. Also make the effort to learn more about the culture of any countries where you may be initiating new relationships, and incorporate this knowledge into your approach. Potential partners will be more receptive to your overtures if they feel that you have taken the time to consider their perspective as well and are interested in a mutually beneficial relationship. (For additional information on international relationships, see Chapter Two.)

Some Simple Steps to Encourage International Interactions

Engaging internationally does not have to start off being complicated or costly, although your approach may evolve over time in ways that may require more resources. The most important consideration initially is positioning your organization to be open to useful information and potential contacts. The examples that follow are of several small organizations that have chosen to take some steps to become more engaged in the international community.

The University of Chicago's David and Alfred Smart Museum of Art, although small, has built a reputation as one of the leading university art museums partly through such international collaborations as exhibitions it has developed with colleagues in other countries, including Korea and China. Many of the contacts that have facilitated these exchanges have been built through university faculty members and colleagues at museums in these countries. The Smart Museum has found that its network of faculty members is a good way to identify opportunities for borrowing collections from overseas to display. This network often helps to identify opportunities that the museum staff then researches (looking at questions such as whether the proposed artwork is in good enough condition to travel) before making final arrangements for an exhibit that will include artwork from overseas. The museum staff has found that using its network to develop good contacts and then taking the time to nurture these contacts has been part of the key to successful exchanges.

Third Sector New England, a Boston-based support group for nonprofits, publishes the nationally circulated *Nonprofit Quarterly* magazine that addresses management issues of critical importance to nonprofits. Third Sector's staff seeks out research and stories that illustrate good practices from both the national and international scene. They believe that the sector as a whole faces common issues and concerns, and the complexity of the problems requires learning from each other's experiences—a necessity for effectiveness.

The Alliance for Community Media, a national membership organization representing public, educational, and governmental access organizations and community media centers, recognized that community media have become common around the world, so it began to reach out to identify people in other countries involved in similar activities. A number of the alliance's members travel as consultants to various countries and now share the information they gain with the organization. The alliance provides an on-line newsletter regarding international developments to facilitate this exchange of information. Other members appreciate being connected to efforts in other countries for community media. These are relatively easy steps that gain for their organizations information of value to their members and constituents.

Networks for Information Exchange

Once you have begun to focus more on international events and trends and your networks reach further, you may identify some existing international networks in your organization's professional field or areas of interest that you might want to join. There are many international networks that already exist, and others are being created regularly.

For example, street papers sold by homeless people (often seen as a local initiative) have sprung up in many places around the world, operating mainly as small nonprofit businesses that give homeless vendors an opportunity to earn a living. The International Network of Street Papers (INSP) began in 1995 to link these local efforts and currently includes papers throughout the world, including the Chicago-based StreetWise and other U.S. organizations. StreetWise personnel made the decision to join this network to have the opportunity to share approaches, concerns, and ideas.

PARENTS FORUM, a Boston-based membership organization that provides networking, skill development, and support to parents and others, had a vision of itself from its beginning as an actor in the international environment. Drawing on the experiences of its board members, PARENTS FORUM looked at a range of network opportunities and identified a few it thought could give it maximum benefit at minimal cost. It currently has links with the Vienna International Committee on the Family, known to several of its board members and offering what the board perceived as affordable membership for a small organization; the Parenting Education and Support Forum of the United Kingdom, also with a reasonable membership fee; the International Federation for Parent Education, through which PARENTS FORUM has been able to participate in ongoing dialogue to develop and expand its network; and CIVICUS, a coalition of NGOs where the PARENTS FORUM has learned about the efforts of other NGOs and has made contacts that have led to a number of mutually beneficial partnerships.

Integrating Lessons from Abroad

Networking and exchanging information with colleagues from other countries may help to strengthen your own local programs and provide solutions or creative ideas to challenges. There are some model practices developed by organizations outside the United States that have real applicability in the United States.

The Women's Self Employment Project (WSEP), a Chicago-based organization to lend women capital to run small businesses, takes as one of its models the Grameen Bank from Bangladesh. The founders of WSEP were looking for some creative alternatives to the traditional training for low-wage jobs that similar programs were involved in when they heard about the Grameen model. They took two essentials from the Grameen model: short-term loans with frequent repayments and organizing women in groups and substituting peer support and pressure (for example, the women did not want to be embarrassed in front of the group if they were not able to pay back the loan) for physical collateral. For the first few years of the program, they followed the Grameen model fairly closely, supported by a visit from the founder of the Grameen Bank. Then they made some modifications to adapt the program to the Chicago environment better, including providing additional flexibility to the number of women in a support group (circle) and providing more business training at the beginning of the program.

WSEP's use of the Grameen model has led to a series of exchanges between the staffs of the two organizations and additional cross-cultural learning experiences. These experiences have influenced the staff of WSEP and women participating in the program to pursue opportunities for exchanging information with counterparts elsewhere in the world, including a video on the business practices of women in Senegal, West Africa.

The National Youth Leadership Council (NYLC), based in St. Paul, Minnesota, draws on the backgrounds of its staff members as well as experiences it has had working in Somali in designing its American-based programs. NYLC is a national nonprofit committed to engaging young people in schools and communities through innovation in learning, leadership, service, and public policy. It has tried to advance a new vision of youth, community, and learning, borrowing from all cultural backgrounds. It shares the belief of many African cultures in the value of the collective group and that true community grows in the hearts of the people who are involved. Based on a successful youth service project completed in Somalia involving consultations with Somalian elders and conversations with national partners who shared their vision of learning and community, NYLC incorporated a Gathering of Elders idea into its annual National Service-Learning Conference as a way to recognize the influential roles that elders play in creating communities of learning that are sustained.

NYLC also incorporated the African art of storytelling, based on a tradition of oral history, into its ten-day youth development camp design and professional development seminars. Conversations are encouraged among key stakeholders of NYLC's national networks by emphasizing relationship building as an essential component to community building.

Management Sciences for Health, based in Boston, applies international lessons to its U.S. health care programs. It has strengthened its management systems based on techniques that were developed overseas and are applicable to U.S. community-based health care groups, sponsored conferences with speakers from other countries, and matched the world of health care professionals in developing countries to the needs of immigrant populations from the same country in the Untied States. Management Sciences tries to identify key issues and then pinpoint tools other cultures are using to address those issues.

Next Steps

If you would like to become more involved in international networking as a way of expanding your organization's international engagement, first establish your goals, and then plan your strategy. If you like the idea of training your board and staff to use global filters and seek out information, provide a checklist like the one shown here that they can use to remind themselves to keep this filter at the forefront of their thinking. Or you might plan to include some small reminders in internal organization communications.

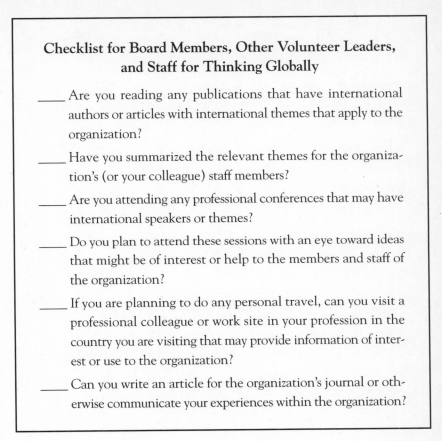

Checklist for Board Members, Other Volunteer Leaders, and Staff for Thinking Globally

_____ Are you reading any publications that have international authors or articles with international themes that apply to the organization?

_____ Have you summarized the relevant themes for the organization's (or your colleague) staff members?

_____ Are you attending any professional conferences that may have international speakers or themes?

_____ Do you plan to attend these sessions with an eye toward ideas that might be of interest or help to the members and staff of the organization?

_____ If you are planning to do any personal travel, can you visit a professional colleague or work site in your profession in the country you are visiting that may provide information of interest or use to the organization?

_____ Can you write an article for the organization's journal or otherwise communicate your experiences within the organization?

Remember to make your international networking efforts an ongoing process. Like starting anything else new, the more you do it, the easier it will become and the more success you will have.

If your networking is progressing well and your organization is ready to move from these informal relationships (information exchange, gathering ideas, joining an international organization in your field) to exploring some more formal cooperative relationships with sister organizations overseas, the next chapter will be of special interest to you.

Chapter Six

Entering the More Formal World of Strategic Alliances and Partnerships

Engaging internationally can start off simply and informally, and it can continue that way for a long time if you are comfortable with this stage. But you may find that your outreach will evolve over time in ways that call for more formal relationships, such as a strategic alliance, with an overseas partner. There are many ways in which such relationships evolve, but two patterns are common. One is that an organization has identified some potential partners through its networking initiatives and through discussions decides it would like to collaborate with an organization in another country on a joint project. In the other, an organization has identified a project it would like to do in another country and seeks a partner to help carry out this project.

An international partnership or alliance may provide a number of benefits to your organization. For example, your organization may gain access to information that is beneficial to its work or to your individual members. It may extend the organization's capabilities and resources and allow it to organize an event overseas (such as a training session or conference) that it may not be able to do on its own. It may help your organization to disseminate its publications. And it may provide an entrée into an international network that can help support its local mission and efforts.

Entering This New Stage: Initial Steps

Although your organization may develop a strategic alliance without going through a networking phase, if your proposed strategic alliance has not resulted from a previous relationship, you

would be well served to take some of the following steps before contemplating a more formal relationship with a potential overseas
partner.

Clarify Organizational Goals

The board should clearly define what it hopes to accomplish by
undertaking an alliance or partner relationship. It can arrive at
this understanding by examining a number of questions:

- What are we looking for in a partner, and what are we willing
  to give?
- Is an alliance or partner relationship the method most suited
  to accomplishing our goals?
- Have we begun to consider some of the advantages and some
  of the challenges we may face?
- How long do we anticipate this relationship lasting? Is it just
  for a specific time-defined project, such as a conference or
  training session, or do we hope that it will be longer lasting?

Conduct Research

If your proposed partnership has not resulted from a previous relationship, it is important to research potential partners before entering a formal agreement. Talk to any contacts you have and trust in
the partner's country about its work and local reputation. Or review
any publicly available information you can locate, such as annual
reports. (Note that what is publicly available may depend on the
country and the regulations for organizations.) This can be similar
to the process of doing a reference check for potential employees or
board members. Stories in the media about the organization may
provide some background information as well. Your partnership
will have the best chance for success if you know something about

how your potential partner operates before you begin to discuss a cooperative relationship.

Evaluate the Importance of Political, Language, and Other Cultural Factors

With each potential partner you identify overseas, evaluate the areas in which it operates differently from your organization. In addition to the types of work style issues you would review for a domestic partnership, look at questions like these:

- If the country of the potential partner is not English speaking, how comfortable are the leaders and staff of the potential partner with working in English or the working language of your organization?
- What is the political relationship between the target country and the United States? For example, will it be difficult for your potential partner's representatives to obtain a visa to the United States or for goods to be shipped through customs?
- Are there cultural differences that may pose obstacles? For example, is your group used to collective, consensus decision making, which may not be a common practice for your potential partner?

Develop Criteria for Choosing Partners

You may want to develop criteria for evaluating potential partners before continuing too far along with your proposed collaboration discussions. Some criteria may be important for any collaboration, such as organizational and governance transparency (so you clearly know who you will be working with), financial stability, or local government approval. Other criteria may be developed that pertain to a specific activity, such as resources within the hospitality industry if the proposed activity is a meeting or conference and the local partner will have responsibilities for the local logistics.

Make Personal Contacts

As we are seeing a growth in options for global communications, there is sometimes the assumption that relationships can be developed by telephone, e-mail, and other technical methods of communication. Although there are undoubtedly successful relationships that develop in this way, never diminish the value of personal contact. Especially when you are operating internationally, you will find that in many cultures, developing an in-person relationship will be key to establishing trust and a successful working relationship.

Once you have established this relationship, communicating by telephone and e-mail can greatly ease your efforts, but relying on technology in the beginning stages of the relationship is not the best way to give the relationship the foundation it needs to grow. (See Chapter Ten for additional discussion on communications.)

Consider the Number and Type of Partners That May Be Most Effective

For some projects, having several partners working together provides the best mixture for a successful project. For example, perhaps no single organization's work is comparable to the work of your organization in the country you would like to do work in, but there are several organizations that can work together, each having some complementary resources. Or it may be important in the target country to have a government entity represented in the partnership. Working with more than one partner also presents a more challenging set of group dynamics. If you have experience with such working groups closer to home, you may feel comfortable entering into a similar arrangement internationally. However, it may not be prudent to try such a relationship for the first time when you are entering a new overseas environment.

Developing the Alliance Agreement

Once you have identified specific goals regarding your new relationships, make sure to clarify these goals and expectations with your potential partners. What resources is your organization willing to allocate to this effort, and what are you expecting of your proposed partner, for example? Be willing to envision the strengths and limitations of each partner. Clarifying these goals and expectations at the early stages of a relationship can help to avoid complications at later stages.

Every organization has its own level of comfort with the degree of formality and legality needed for a partnership agreement. The activity you propose to undertake will also provide parameters for what an agreement should include. For example, if the agreement is primarily an exchange of information, a less formal letter of agreement might suffice. However, if significant financial resources will be committed, a more formal contract will be important. Such an agreement should cover issues such as copyright and intellectual property protection for any items you may be exchanging and a termination clause. If you are to enter a formal contractual relationship, be sure to consult an attorney who has experience with the country of your partner organization. (See Chapter Eleven for a further discussion of legal issues.)

There are various reasons for entering a collaborative arrangement. You may want to facilitate a specific project or have an ongoing relationship that will help your organization establish a presence in a particular part of the world or accomplish other long-term goals. Or you may want to start with a specific project and then consider a longer-term relationship if it goes well. Defining the scope of the project will be important to finding the right partner whose expectations meet yours and to providing a way to bring the relationship to an amiable close when that time comes.

Take the time to develop a relationship with your proposed partner. During this initial period, you can learn much about how it operates and how you can work together. One important way of developing this relationship is to work together with your partner organization to outline the tasks that each of you will undertake. The process of working through your individual roles and responsibilities will help to clarify the relationship and identify any potential challenges in working together. By doing this early in the relationship, you can make modifications in your approach when it is still early enough in the process to do so and allow each partner a way to gracefully withdraw if necessary (the concept of saving face is especially important in some cultures).

Developing some oversight and monitoring mechanisms is important so that each partner knows if the other is adhering to the terms of the agreement. Identify the key contact people working on the project on a day-to-day basis and which more senior people may need to be drawn in if there are complications with implementing particular parts of the plan.

At the end of your collaborative project (or initial project if you hope others will follow), evaluate the collaboration to see if it met the expectations of each partner. An evaluation at the end of the project requires developing some framework for judging it. This activity will also help in clarifying the expectations of each partner. Develop a checklist or another type of short form with items that can be kept in mind as the organizers plan the joint event or work on the collaborative project. Having such expectations in writing can also help to avoid misunderstandings that may arise from difficulties with language or differing cultural perceptions. (See the sample monitoring and evaluation checklist on page 67.)

No matter how much you try to anticipate, working internationally often means learning to live with ambiguity and adjusting as circumstances change. Be prepared to enter partnerships with a willingness to adapt to change. You will also want a partner that is willing to be flexible and to compromise. For example, be wary of partners that are overly concerned about maintaining authority over the project and create competitive situations or power struggles.

Sample Monitoring and Evaluation Checklist

_____ Are the roles for each partner clear?

_____ Has each partner accepted its responsibilities?

_____ Is there a mechanism or process for articulating and modifying any changes that a partner might want to make in its agreed responsibilities or assigned tasks?

_____ Are lines of communication clear? (In some countries respecting protocol and seniority is very important.)

_____ Have timetables for accomplishing each partner's tasks been agreed to?

_____ Do the partners have the same approach to due dates?

_____ What action can a partner take if the due dates for the other partner slip?

_____ Will any of these agreements or other materials need translation?

_____ How does each partner define a successful outcome for the collaboration?

_____ By what process will the collaboration be evaluated?

_____ Are you publicizing the collaboration to your members and within your organization's network? (Publicizing the collaboration may help to identify other opportunities that can come from this initial endeavor.)

Partnering for a Specific Activity or Project

The following two organizations have developed strategic alliances for a specific activity or project in another country: one of them a conference and the other providing professional training opportunities.

The Association for Volunteer Administration (AVA) was approached by an organization in Korea to cosponsor a regional

Asia-Pacific event on volunteer administration. Over the course of a three-year exchange of communication, AVA agreed to cooperate on such an event. The initial communication was by e-mail, and then a Korean delegation came to AVA's annual conference to discuss in person the idea of a regional conference. A letter of agreement outlined the responsibilities of each organization after both felt comfortable that they could work with the other. The Korean organization did the local organizing and found local sponsors. AVA provided its expertise on program development and its name as a cosponsor, and it helped to publicize the event. Both organizations viewed the event as a successful collaboration.

The Community Leadership Association (CLA), an organization of six hundred community-based leadership programs sponsored by a university or chamber of commerce, based in Indianapolis, has pursued local linkages to deliver training programs in different countries. In Thailand, for example, CLA worked with a local economic development group, a business group (similar to a chamber of commerce), and local universities. Based on an initial discussion of goals and needs of the training, CLA staff prepared a draft curriculum and participant materials that all of the organizing groups reviewed. The Thai groups provided CLA with a written overall evaluation, including areas to improve or amend the curriculum and other materials. They also helped find local participants, sponsors, and translators.

The initial projects were deemed successful, and CLA proceeded to the next level of training with the same local partners. Among the keys to the success of the project of the project were these:

- Securing adequate funding from local and international sources
- Having established partners who could help implement the project locally and sustain it
- Taking into account cultural expectations and considerations
- Being open to change and adaptability and learning from the local partners

Partnerships for Developing Local Capacity

In 1999, after more than one hundred years of service in the United States, the national board of Volunteers of America (VOA) approved the extension of its work beyond U.S. borders. The leadership determined the best course of expansion to be through collaborative ventures with indigenous partners, reasoning that deference should be given to local direction, a principle that underlies the organization's success in the United States; resources should not be spent on duplication of effort; and serving people most in need could best be achieved by helping to build skills that lead to self-sufficiency. In 2001, VOA had an opportunity to partner with a small nonprofit meeting the criteria, Mano La Paz ("Hands for Peacemaking"). Mano La Paz works with Mayan Indians in community development projects throughout the remote Guatemalan highlands of Huehuetenango. An agreement to partner was the first step in working together, with the ultimate goal being the establishment of a new joint venture in Guatemala.

Although the joint venture would be jointly controlled by the two parent organizations, it would be a separate legal entity. This type of alliance is more complex than other partnership agreements, but it protects the assets of each organization because the partners are legally independent of each other. Mano La Paz benefits from the association with one of the largest human service agencies in the United States. VOA reduces its risk exposure by collaborating with an established in-country partner. Both organizations benefit by pooling resources to gain economies of scale and avoid competition.

A year later, although the joint venture was still being refined, capacity building and programmatic initiatives were under way. The first country director for Mano La Paz was the first participant in the VOA Global Fellowship Program, which invites emerging civil society leaders from around the world to join with VOA in an interdisciplinary executive education program in nonprofit management at a U.S. university. VOA has also received funding from the U.S. Department of State to host an exchange program between the United States and Guatemala for health care and social service professionals working with people with disabilities.

The key lessons learned in the process of developing this alliance echo many outlined in this chapter:

- Choice of partner is very important, and relationships are not built quickly.
- An up-front resource commitment is necessary to ensure adequate communication and representation in planning initiatives.
- All partners need flexibility to adjust to changing circumstances and agility to respond to new opportunities.
- Have a written agreement detailing the parameters of the partnership.

Chapter Seven

Considering Other Possible International Program Ideas

The previous chapters have explored some of the paths most often taken by nonprofit organizations as they expand their vision outward into the world: using their meetings and annual conferences, international networking, and developing partnership relationships. This chapter looks at a few more of the many paths that are open to you. You are limited only by your organization's own imagination and global entrepreneurship.

Giving Birth to a New Program

Your organization may have an idea for a program that it would like to try that will engage it internationally, but you are not sure exactly how it will develop. An effective way to try out this idea is to nurture it along with available resources until you are sure that it can take on a greater prominence in your organization. Perhaps the turning point for greater prominence will be a funder who is interested in providing financial resources for the project, a well-known figure who is interested in supporting your vision, or simply a group of interested members of your international network that will provide the foundation this envisioned program may need to link and grow internationally. If you become committed to the value of an international program to your organization, be ready with a strong foundation for the program in place, including your organization's leadership and the staff's understanding of their roles in the overall organizational mission when such an opportunity comes along. Remember the lessons of Chapter Three: to be sustainable, this international program growth must be compatible with your organization's mission.

Consider the experience of Boston-based City Year. City Year brings together young people ages seventeen to twenty-four from diverse economic, racial, and geographical backgrounds for a year of full-time service in civic engagement and service to communities across the country. City Year, which began in Boston in the late 1980s and has grown to include programs throughout the country, started with a goal of being a key driver of the movement for a national service system (which did not exist in the late 1980s).

Since its inception, City Year has received visitors from all over the world interested in launching citizen service initiatives in their countries. City Year also has integrated ideas from other countries and cultures into its own program. The use of ideas from other cultures is a method of having myths or founding stories as touchstones for perspective, understanding, and inspiration. For example, proverbs from different cultures (such as "Consider the effects of your actions on seven generations") are used to stimulate participants' knowledge of the past and how it links to their present and future actions in the community.

Further developing these interests and with the support of former President Bill Clinton, City Year launched the Clinton Democracy Fellowship in 2001 to build a global network of young leaders between the ages of twenty-one and thirty-five in emerging and established democracies who are committed to developing citizen service programs, advancing citizen service policy, and using social entrepreneurship techniques to strengthen democracy. In addition to providing learning opportunities to young leaders from other countries, City Year sees this program as an opportunity for Americans to learn from young leaders engaged in democracy building around the world.

The Center for Civic Education (founded as the Los Angeles Center for Civic Education) is an organization that has broadened its mandate to encompass first the state of California, then the nation, and eventually the international arena. Founded in 1964 at the University of California, Los Angeles (UCLA) to develop innovative curricula, the project went statewide in 1969 and became an independent nonprofit organization in 1981. The center administers a wide range of curricula, teacher training, and community-based programs specializing in civic and citizenship education.

Beginning in the 1970s, the center participated in cooperative exchange programs with the Federal Center for Political Exchange of the Federal Republic of Germany. The programs involved one-week seminars on civic education held in the United States and Germany in alternating years. In the late 1980s, with the changing political situation in Eastern Europe and the former Soviet Union, there was an increased interest in democracy and a call for the center's curricular resources and programs. In 1995, building on its successful international initiative with Germany, the center applied for and received funding from the U.S. Department of Education for a new program, Civitas: An International Civic Education Exchange Program. This program provides for a series of exchanges among leaders in civic education in the United States and emerging and established democracies worldwide. The center is now supported in its international initiatives by its mission, which was revised to call for supporting "active citizenship in the U.S. and other countries."

Catalyst for Collective Action

Sometimes an organization can serve as a catalyst for collective action, allowing a group to do something in the international arena that it might not do on their own. The Council of Great Lakes Governors is a nonprofit organization based in Chicago that represents the eight governors of states surrounding the Great Lakes. In the late 1980s, the states began discussing the possibility of opening a collective trade office and explored various other countries where companies in their states were doing business or interested in expanding their business. In 1990, based partially on relationships that had been established by the council working with the province of Ontario on issues affecting the Great Lakes, four of the states agreed to open a trade office in Toronto, Canada, together. The success of this office eventually led to the opening of four more joint offices in Argentina, Brazil, Chile, and South Africa later in the decade.

Dedicated Staff to International Programming

Your organization may want to do more to sustain and institutionalize your growing window on the world but allow it the flexibility to grow and evolve as your organization does. An effective pattern is often to start small, with just a percentage of a staff person's time dedicated to international initiatives, and extend the dedicated staff time as needed, perhaps increasing it to one full-time person, or adding additional staff members as the program grows. Remember the lessons of Chapter Three: to be most effective, this type of progression should happen in a deliberate and measured way, expanding only when the organization is clearly ready and able. In many cases, this growth will take place over a number of years. And to be sustainable, this international program growth must be compatible with your organization's mission.

Consider the example of BoardSource (originally the National Center for Nonprofit Boards). In the mid-1990s, BoardSource, which had been focused primarily on domestic nonprofits and their local and national issues, began to see an increased interest and awareness concerning the importance of the role of boards from NGOs around the world.

BoardSource started a small international program, dedicating one staff person to explore this possibility and develop a program for the organization. The organization initiated a number of one-to-one partnerships to formulate new approaches to strengthening the governance of NGOs. Cooperative projects included jointly publishing new materials in the local language and adapted to nonprofits locally in several parts of the world and cosponsoring training sessions. It also initiated a fellows program to bring nonprofit organization professionals from around the world to its annual conference.

These programs were so successful that five years later, BoardSource had a dedicated consulting staff to provide consulting for nonprofit and nongovernmental organizations throughout the world. It had expanded its focus worldwide, noting on its Web site that due to the "increasing importance of the role of nonprofit organizations worldwide, BoardSource has become a global resource on nonprofit governance."

Lessons from the Examples

These examples show that an incremental approach to international activity is often the most effective. Start with an approach that feels most comfortable for your organization at the time. This initiative can then be nurtured until you are sure that your leadership is ready to give it (and internationalism) a greater prominence in your organization.

There are many different paths to increasing your organization's international engagement. Be open to opportunities that may present themselves, and be creative about the way in which you introduce a window on the world to your organizations.

Part Three

International Operational Issues

Chapter Eight

Bringing International Members into Your Decision-Making Groups

If your organization is ready to take an important next operational step in becoming more international, look at the composition of your committees and board and other volunteer leadership positions. Are these positions as accessible to non-U.S. participants as they are to those who reside in the United States? Is your organization representing its non-U.S. members and constituents in its decision-making process? Is it benefiting from the varied perspectives that non-U.S. participants can bring to your decision-making bodies?

Although boards and committees play different roles in the governance of an organization—boards being responsible for policy and fiscal stability and committees providing advice or accomplishing specific program tasks—most of the comments in this chapter apply to both boards and committee groups. (If they apply specifically to one group or the other, this is noted.)

The Benefits of Multinational Boards and Committees

Bringing non-U.S. members or representatives of other constituent groups that your organization serves onto your board and other volunteer committees can provide a number of benefits. A diversified board or committee creates a broad-based prism for viewing the world, helping to identify and analyze international trends that may affect the organization. At the same time, it sends the message within your organization, to the community you are working to serve, to your donors and other partners, and to the international community that your organization is truly committed to international engagement. If you are a membership organization, these opportunities provide international members the chance to be represented in the organization's decision-making structure.

International members provide learning opportunities about international issues and perspectives to all members of the board and committee, and they bring new ideas to the organization. Depending on your goals, having international board or committee members can provide access to decision makers or the media in other countries.

The rationale for bringing non-U.S. members or representatives of other constituent groups that your organization serves into your leadership positions depends on how your organization currently makes decisions about its operations. If it is mission based, this will help ensure that the perspectives of those using your services are reflected in planning and operations; certainly your organization should have representatives of the communities being served in your leadership. In a business-based organization, the leadership should include individuals who bring contacts and knowledge related to the communities served. And in an organization based on the responsible "community citizen," having representatives of the international community in your leadership will help you to forward this goal and become a more effective citizen of the world community of NGOs.

One analysis in the corporate literature looks at multinational companies at three stages of internationalizing their corporate decision making: ethnocentric, polycentric, and geocentric.[1] The ethnocentric multinational firm is characterized by a home country orientation. It is primarily a domestic firm with some foreign extensions; managerial positions are reserved for home country executives. In the polycentric multinational firm, local managers are put in charge of local operations, but high-level executive positions are still reserved for home country executives. It is only in the geocentric multinational firm that these home country biases are overcome, and the company demonstrates that it values diversity and begins to multinationalize its board. More recent studies of multinational firms continue to show these patterns.

Some useful parallels with this analysis can be drawn for the nonprofit sector. Where is your organization on the internationalizing spectrum in Figure 1.1, and where along the spectrum would you like to move toward? If you are primarily a U.S. organization that is just starting to integrate some non-U.S. participants into your decision-making process, you may have a similar approach to the ethnocentric multinational. If you are comfortable at this side of the spectrum, you may not want or need to diversify your decision-making groups. However, if you would like to move along the spectrum, you might consider a geocentric approach, shifting your organization's global mind-set to begin to integrate more global perspectives into the organization's program development and other decision making. There are many benefits to such an approach beyond the most commonly heard reason of providing a greater representation of your membership or constituency groups.

How to Diversify Your Board or Committees

There are a number of ways your organization might diversify its board geographically.

One way is to seek out new board or committee recruits from among your international contacts. (See Chapter Five on networking for ideas on how to extend the organization's outreach and identify those from other countries who are interested in the work of your organization.) This will depend on how your organization's board and committees are selected, but if a nominating committee is used, the committee could add geographical representation to the other characteristics it considers for nominating board or committee candidates.

You can clearly articulate your policy of inclusion in the charge to the nominating committee—for example, "In line with our commitment that our leadership reflect the larger international community we are part of, we will strive to have board and committee membership reflect this."

The committee structure is another route to bring in new leaders who can be nurtured and trained for board positions. Working on a committee can provide the non-U.S. participant an opportunity to see how effective he or she can be working for the organization, and the organization's leadership can assess the effectiveness of this participant. Beginning by serving on a committee can be especially helpful to leadership candidates who are not as familiar with organizations that operate in the United States.

When your organization is seeking non-U.S. members for committees and the board, let it be known throughout your international network, your membership, and any forums in which you might look for potential board and committee members. If an organization commits to offering equal opportunities and non-U.S. members are made to feel welcome and feel they can effectively contribute, more people will come forward, and additional names will be suggested. Those who are already involved will want to stay involved and help recruit others (either formally or informally by word of mouth) from their area of the world.

As you seek new members, it is important to provide candidates with information on the board or committee service and clarify expectations before they agree to be a candidate. Although this is important for any new board or committee member, it is especially important for those who may not have participated before on U.S.-based boards or committees and may have expectations based on experiences in other countries. Briefing them before they accept a position will help to maximize the chances that they will have a positive experience. If you have current board or committee members from outside the United States, ask them what type of information they wish they had had before they began their terms.

Provide supplementary orientation materials to new board or committee members from outside the United States, in addition to the orientation you may provide to all board or committee members. For instance, you may want to include definitions of terms or acronyms commonly used in your meetings. Do not assume that terms that are commonly used in the United States (such as

---

Ideas for Diversifying the Board and Committees

- As board members, staff, and other influential people in the organization travel, ask them to keep an eye out for potential leaders, and encourage them to put the names of these people forward for leadership positions.

- Look to overseas chapters or other local units for leaders who can be encouraged to move higher in the organization.

- Ask current board or committee members from other countries to encourage their qualified colleagues to put their names forward for leadership positions.

- Consider including geographical diversity as one criterion when the nominating committee is developing a slate of candidates.

- Let others in your organization's external network know you are looking for potential leaders from around the world.

501(c)) or acronyms such as EPA are well known worldwide. Current board or committee members from outside the United States can be good sources for the types of information that are helpful to new members. This is especially important for board service where members have fiduciary responsibilities by state and national laws within the United States, which are not necessarily the same in other countries.

Organizational Challenges That Come with Multinational Boards and Committees

For an organization to create smoothly functioning multinational boards and committees that effectively incorporate members from different countries, some effort should be committed to recognizing and addressing the special challenges involved. Each board member from another country brings his or her own cultural background, perspectives, and sets of experiences and needs. Addressing some of the issues that may arise (including cultural and language differences, travel costs, and communication options) as your board is just beginning to have more international members can help to minimize the risk of problems developing later.

Language Differences

Although English has become the language of international business and many organizations choose to use it as their common language, board or committee members who speak English as an additional language may not be as comfortable functioning in English as their board or committee colleagues who have English as their native tongue. Native English-speaking board or committee members must understand the need to speak slowly and clearly and avoid the use of acronyms or jargon. The board or committee chair must be especially aware of the need to ensure that everyone is following the discussion and stop periodically to summarize, clarify, or allow "whisper translations" from one board or committee member to another. The board or committee may establish a practice of having as many materials as possible available in writing, which will make it easier for non-native English speakers to follow the discussions.

Travel Costs

Bringing non-U.S. members on your board or committees requires a commitment to including them as equal partners. This means that if your organization has a policy of subsidizing travel for board or committee members, you will need to have the financial resources to provide for international travel as well. Some organizations try to maximize the benefits from travel costs by scheduling board or committee meetings to coincide with their annual conference or another professional meeting that a majority of the board or committee members are planning on attending. If you are considering scheduling such a meeting, you might want to weigh the advantages (cost and travel time) against the potential disadvantages (lack of focus, fatigue that comes from attending back-to-back meetings) before making the decision.

If the cost of bringing together a group from different countries is cost prohibitive for your organization, consider setting up an international advisory council. This group can advise your board and staff on international developments and trends of interest to your organization but can operate by telephone or e-mail rather than attending meetings in person. If your organization has an annual conference that attracts non-U.S. attendees, consider scheduling an international advisory group meeting around the time of the conference. (See Chapter Four on meetings for more ideas on maximizing conference opportunities.)

Communication Channels

Having non-U.S. board members or committee members can increase your organization's costs of communicating, but it does not need to be cost prohibitive. The key to effective international communication is ensuring that everyone feels they have adequate and equal opportunities to participate. These opportunities do not all have to be identical, but they should provide equal access.

An attitude of inclusion, which has no monetary cost, can be as important as any financial expenditures your organization may make. Especially if your board or committees are primarily from the United States, all members of the group should be sensitive to ensuring inclusion of the non-U.S. members. For example, if your board or committee chooses to do a lot of its communication by e-mail, a fairly cost-effective mechanism, be careful that the discussion does not advance too far toward reaching a decision before a board or committee member who lives in a part of the world where it is the middle of the night while this discussion is going on has a chance to see how the discussion has evolved. (See Chapter Ten for more information on communication.)

Leadership

The leaders of an organization must believe in the importance of internationalism and work to translate this belief into their everyday actions and decisions. Current global structures encourage nationalism, not internationalism. Cultural, ethnic, religious, and increasingly regional groupings also have played a role in the way that individuals define their identity, thereby influencing their decision making and potential differences among board members. Leaders need to believe in the benefits that internationalism brings, to be visionary and motivational, and to lead sometimes skeptical constituencies to put the entire organization's interests above that of any one interest group. In addition, leaders must strive to be good team leaders, even if their cultural background may not easily point them in this direction.

Training

As you become more internationally engaged, your top elected leaders will become international ambassadors for the organization. In addition to their internal interactions with colleague board members, members, and staff, they will begin to interact with leaders of counterpart or affiliated organizations in other countries or leaders in international organizations. You may want to consider a global awareness training session, perhaps as part of a board orientation session, that focuses on international protocols and practices and cultural sensitivity.

Challenges to Individual Board and Committee Members

In addition to the collective challenges to the organization of having effective and smoothly functioning multinational decision-making groups, there are also individual challenges to each member who serves on these groups. By focusing on how his or her actions can be adapted to working with a multinational set of peers, each member can help the group to work better as a unit.

Cultural Styles

Each culture has its unique characteristics. For a multinational board or committee to operate effectively, there must be a high level of tolerance. When a colleague's verbal presentation or decision-making process appears bewildering or counterproductive to another, the organization will be best served if the board or committee member does not prejudge this person without first striving to understand his or her background or cultural approach. For example, some Asian cultures consider it rude to disagree in a direct way, but silence may not signify agreement. It will be important to find ways for these disagreements to be delivered and interpreted in more subtle ways. Some board or committee members may understand more than one culture and would be willing to serve as cultural interpreters.

Global Perspective

A member of an international board or committee needs to think globally. Each board member (as in a single-nation organization) brings his or her own experiences to the table, which lends an important diversity to the discussions. However, in an international organization, it is especially important for all board or committee members to base their decisions on the welfare of the entire organization, not just the needs of their own national constituency. When individual board or committee members lapse into parochialism, they can jeopardize the commitment to the core values that are essential for an organization committed to internationalism to operate effectively.

Communication

If there are board or committee members whose native language is not English, those who are more comfortable with English need to be understanding of members who may find it challenging to operate in a foreign language. Speaking slowly, minimizing the use of acronyms and colloquial expressions, and being willing to stop periodically to summarize or explain are all approaches that will help those who are not as comfortable with English to feel an equal member of the board or committee. (See Chapter Ten for further discussion of communication issues.)

Examples of Leadership Integration Efforts

The Community Leadership Association (CLA) began to groom new board members by seeking out non-U.S. members for committee work to learn more about CLA and how it operates. It used its Board Development Committee to look at a variety of board demographics, including country identification, and to encourage diversity. As its program in international training grew, it sought ways to bring on more international board members to help the organization design and understand these training opportunities. A major challenge was to do this within a limited budget, and alternative ways to conduct the board's business, such as fewer meetings and fewer board members, were explored.

As the International Association of Jazz Education (IAJE) began expanding its membership outside the United States, it made a commitment to providing a seat on the board for each part of the world that had a core group of members. Initially, the primary challenge was to integrate members from other countries successfully into what had been a U.S.-focused organization. A major component to this effort was a strategic planning process that modeled what they hoped their future decision-making process would look like. A non-U.S. board member was a cochair of the strategic planning committee, and each of the strategic planning process task forces had non-U.S. members. This process enabled IAJE's leaders to integrate international colleagues and perspectives into all aspects of their decision-making process.

Chapter Nine

Expanding Your International Reach Through Your Membership

Whether you have actively recruited international members or if they have just found their way to your organization, having a membership outside the United States requires some special planning. The expectations of these members may be different from those of your U.S. members, and the mechanisms you have developed that successfully serve your U.S. members may not be as appropriate to members outside of the country.

If you are actively recruiting membership, look at what your organization hopes to accomplish in developing your non-U.S. membership. There is a variety of reasons for expanding international membership, including providing global leadership in your field, broadening the horizons of your U.S. members, enhancing your organization's image and prestige (which can also lead to increased influence in areas such as policy), and disseminating the goals and services of your organization more widely.

But there are also costs to servicing and maintaining an international membership, so ask some of the following questions before you begin an international expansion:

- What reasons do you have to go international?
- What similar organizations may exist in other countries or worldwide? How will your role be different from theirs?
- Who would you like to have as members? Why?
- How will you develop this program?
- How will you manage it?

What costs are you willing to absorb to recruit and retain an international membership? Determine how much your organization is willing to subsidize international growth versus how much it wants to meet costs. Generating matching funds and revenue can take time. Some long-term possibilities for meeting costs might include developing cooperative relationships with partner countries to provide funding for an overseas educational program or having enough members from a particular country that you can serve them at a return that covers your cost. But these returns on your investment will take time. You need to anticipate and budget some initial seed funding.

Differing Expectations of Domestic and International Members

The expectations of members from different parts of the world may vary from those of your U.S. members, and your organization will have to consider how it will meet these expectations. Anticipating and planning for these differences of perspective from the beginning of the recruitment process can aid in the retention rate of new members from other countries. As with your domestic members, it can be more costly to an organization to constantly bring in new members who do not remain members for very long than commit what is needed to retain members.

Which services are of most interest to your nonlocal members that will provide the greatest return in these members' feeling truly part of the organization? Take time to ask your members what their expectations and needs are and how the services you already provide are responding to those needs. Interests often vary depending on a member's geographical location. For example, non-U.S. members will have limited interest in U.S. regulatory or tax-exempt issues or awards that are available only to U.S. citizens. Look at a full range of membership services and responsibilities, including international representation on your board and other committees, dues fees and payments, publications distribution, and how annual conferences are organized. Making your services accessible to those outside the United States is more than just a matter of translating your materials into another language.

Conduct an international assessment (as described in Chapter Two) periodically to ensure that your full range of services are being designed with an international membership in mind. Some services may be of more interest and applicability to some areas of the world than others, and you may want to offer different options. You may need to phase in a broader multicultural appeal. Conducting an international assessment will provide the information you need to make educated decisions and your leadership the evidence it needs to explain its decisions to members. On an ongoing basis, you should monitor the satisfaction of international members and respond to their concerns. For example, monitor that your mailings overseas are not being unduly delayed. Timely services may come with a cost to the organization, but the return in member retention may be great.

Some members may have come to your organization because there was no equivalent organization in their country or internationally. But as more NGOs start up around the world, you may need to work harder to show the value of membership in your organization. Make sure your organization is offering services or benefits to international constituents that are not available to them on a local or national level.

Adapting Membership Services
to International Members

There are some basic modifications to consider in adapting membership services to international members.

Databases

Make sure your databases are accessible to non-English names and non-American addresses. Take the time to understand how names are written and should be recorded in the parts of the world where you have members. For example, Chinese names are customarily written with the family name first and then the given name.

Time Zones

Make sure your staff realizes the ramifications of different time zones around the world. For example, if you are calling a member in another country or scheduling a conference call, make sure you take time differences into consideration. No one appreciates a call in the middle of their night. If you are planning a conference call and one member of the group is taking that call early in the morning or late at night, consider rotating this inconvenience for the next call.

Mailings

There are often trade-offs between how much you spend on sending mail and how long it will take to reach its destination. Review the options for sending publications and other communications to members, and monitor how long they are taking to reach their destination (which is sometimes different from the advertised time frames). With this information, you can then decide on an acceptable option considering your budget and members' needs and expectations.

To minimize shipping time and cost, many organization are now considering and using more electronic communications. Although access to the Internet has spread widely around the world, this access is still costly or limited or unreliable in various parts of the world. If your members do have easy access to electronic communication, you may want to consider a virtual membership option, which is discussed later in this chapter.

Translations

Identify when translations may or may not be necessary so you do not have to absorb costs that may not be needed. Although translations are helpful in many situations, they may not always be necessary, and there may be more cost-effective alternatives to meeting your goals. For example, if your goal at a meeting is to have a small number of attendees who are not fluent in English be able to follow the proceedings, consider having as many presentations as possible available to attendees in writing, which is easier to follow, instead of investing in full simultaneous interpretation.

Web Site

Many organizations are finding Web sites a valuable way to provide information and communicate with members. As your Web site strategy evolves, review its design and content through your global filter, making sure that it is equally accessible and appealing to overseas members as to domestic members. This may include ideas such as incorporating more drawings, diagrams, and other graphic information that will be useful to those who do not read English (or the language of your Web site) well; translating some sections into other languages; or making other changes recommended by members from outside the United States.

Accessible Services

Making services accessible to those outside the United States is more than just a question of translating into another language (although translation may be important in some cases as well). An international assessment will provide information as to how accessible your products and services are to members from other countries. If there are gaps, consider ways to make your publications and other products of greater interest to members from other countries. Some of these ideas do not necessarily involve great cost but rather a greater ongoing attention to how your products are perceived by your international members. Or if few international members can afford to attend your annual conference, consider some distance learning options or some smaller educational programs in an overseas location where you have a group of members or other partner that can help you to organize this.

Opportunities for Leadership Roles

For international members to feel that they are equal members of the organization and to sustain their involvement, they must have equal opportunities with domestic members to gain leadership roles. Develop a clear policy of inclusion, and publicize it throughout your membership that your organization is seeking non-U.S. members for committees and the board. If your organization commits to offering equal opportunities and non-U.S. members are made to feel welcome and feel they can effectively contribute, more people will come forward, and international members will feel more vested in the organization.

Other Services

Other ideas to consider for international members range from sections in your newsletter or journal that are devoted to international trends in your field or member profiles (this can also be a benefit to your U.S. members) to mailings that are customized to take into consideration the special interests of non-U.S. members and special services such as detailed orientation materials, currency exchange, or translation at your annual meetings.

Organizing the International Membership

Your headquarters operations and local components are equally valuable parts of the network. International networks are only as strong as their component parts and need to stay close to their membership or local partners. An international network can add value if common issues and a collective purpose are identified. There are numerous options to consider for organizing your international membership.

Existing models generally vary depending on choice of how much independence local entities will have and range from limited independence (well-integrated chapters) to complete independence (allied partners and alliances). The needs and types of goods and services desired by members or constituent groups can vary considerably by location. Your organization should decide what is core to its mission that all units must share or be responsible for and what can vary according to location.

There are a variety of organizational options. This outline looks at four common ones and some of the trade-offs to consider. Note that structures can change over time as the organization grows and changes, although it is most efficient not to restructure too often. In addition, some of growth and need for change can be anticipated and planned for.

Chapters

Because this option has traditionally been the most common for membership organizations in the United States, many organizations have continued this structure when they have grown internationally. Chapters (sometimes also called clubs) are an integral part of the parent organization and operate in close cooperation with headquarters. The major advantage for the parent organization is accountability: strict reporting of all activities or key areas. The major advantage for the chapter is support: financial and in-kind support.

In some organizations, chapters can have independent incorporation and be responsible for their own budgets. If you are considering such a structure, discuss the financial and legal advantages and disadvantages with legal counsel.

An example of an organization that uses the chapter structure is the Association of Fundraising Professionals (AFP), which started in the United States in 1960. Liked-minded groups of fundraising professionals formed chapters in Toronto in 1970 and Mexico City in 1993. In 1996, the organization's strategic planning committee determined that it should be a North American organization and created the Canadian Initiative Task Force with members from across Canada and some key leaders in the United States.

Its focus was to develop chapters in Canada; eventually, nine were started in Canadian cities. With the success of the Canadian Initiative Task Force, a similar task force was created in Mexico. It faced greater challenges due to language differences and the laws regulating the incorporation of chapters in Mexico, but it did successfully nurture additional chapters in Mexico. All chapters receive the same benefits, although there are legal differences in how they are structured.

Another example of an organization that uses this structure is the Make-A-Wish Foundation (MAWF) International. Make-A-Wish Foundation of America was founded in 1980 and by 1993 had generated enough interest around the world that the Make-A-Wish Foundation International was officially formed as an affiliation of the five founding country associations that were already granting wishes. MAWF International, headquartered in Arizona, had twenty-seven chapters (also called affiliates) around the world by 2002. Each of these groups shares core values, and policies and guidelines outline the responsibilities of the local group and those of MAWF International. The international goals include establishing basic principles to ensure that the highest standards of ethics and conduct are uniformly followed and adhered to by affiliated charities that are members of the Make-A-Wish family throughout the world; encourage planned growth of the wish-granting concept in receptive countries; and provide advice and consultation among its affiliates.

Affiliates

This option is often used when members in a particular country prefer their own local organization to provide member services and carry out local programs and grants a fair amount of autonomy for the local group. It works best when there is an agreement between the affiliates and the international organization as to the benefits they derive and their responsibilities.

Sister Cities International (SCI) uses this structure. SCI works to promote cultural understanding, social development, and economic growth by facilitating educational exchanges, business development opportunities, and information across borders from city to city. It is a national membership organization that officially certifies links between U.S. communities and those overseas. SCI has as its members U.S. cities, counties, states, and territories, as well as international communities that have a recognized sister city relationship with a U.S. community. The SCI network represents more than twenty-one hundred communities in 121 countries around the world that operate independently to forward SCI's mission. In addition, corporations, associations, educational institutions, individuals, and other donors are invited to become part of the sister cities network as nonvoting members. A commitment to the core mission of the organization is ensured by the fact that members are communities, and the sister city relationships must be formally approved by the governing body of the local government.

Electronic or Virtual Membership

Benefits and services are delivered exclusively electronically in electronic membership. This is often seen as beneficial to both the organization and the international membership because it reduces the time and cost of sending publications. For example, the Percussive Arts Society (PAS) has an on-line membership category that includes all of its standard membership benefits, including discounts on many of the organization's products and services; however, ePAS members do not receive printed copies of the organization's two regular publications. Both of those publications are included in their entirety on the organization's Web site, from which entire issues or individual articles can be downloaded. This membership option is also made more attractive by the breadth of options offered electronically, including participation in chat groups, education sessions, committees and other volunteer activities, search options for percussive information, and access to information twenty-four hours a day, seven days a week for members in all time zones. The electronic membership fee is also less than half of the regular membership option.

Hybrid

Based on some strategic planning discussions that reviewed the approach PAS would take in growing internationally, the organization adopted several options—chapters, affiliation, or an alliance—that it would make available to its international members. The chapter option, PAS's traditional structure, is provided to international member groups that want to be an integral part of the organization. Active chapters must comply with all PAS bylaws and policies. An affiliate member organization is an option open to an independent national organization that wants a close relationship with PAS. Affiliates are linked to PAS by Web sites, an optional annual affiliate event, and by providing an active membership mailing list to PAS annually. An alliance membership is open to an independent national organization that wants a relationship with PAS as agreed to be mutually beneficial.

Many of PAS's agreements with its affiliate and alliance partners have focused on the support of conventions and special events. PAS has traded advertising of special events and had a display or someone from PAS promoting the organization at these events. It has stayed flexible in developing agreements suitable to the specific partner relationships. Many of the organization's initial relationships are in Europe, with developing relationships in Asia and South America.

Like PAS, the Association of Fundraising Professionals looked at other options for existing organizations to be affiliated with it as it began to expand internationally. AFP did not want to jeopardize relationships with existing fundraising organizations around the world, so the strategy of developing strategic alliances was formed.

In this way, if a country did not have an existing fundraising organization, an AFP chapter could be formed, but if there was already an organization meeting the needs of fundraising professionals in a country, AFP would develop an arrangement with those other organizations.

The first two alliances were formed in 2002 with strategic alliances with the Institute of Fundraising in the United Kingdom and the Fundraising Institute of Australia and a third in 2003 with the Fundraising Institute of New Zealand. These arrangements allow for members of one of the groups to opt in to a Web-based membership with AFP and for the same option to be available to members of AFP, with AFP's overseas partners. This Web-based membership provides access to the members-only area of the others' Web sites, electronic newsletters, and member discounts to attend the others' conferences. The cooperation agreements also provide other reciprocal benefits to the organizations, including information exchange in a variety of programmatic and technical areas and observer status to meetings of the others' governing bodies.

Governance Structure

As your international membership grows, a major part of your decisions on structure will encompass how the organization can best include these members in its governance. These issues should be considered as part of your ongoing strategic planning efforts (see Chapter Three on integrating international perspectives into your strategic planning initiatives).

Good governance of nonprofit organizations means that nonprofit board members understand their job and carry out their responsibilities. This includes ensuring that the organization's mission is appropriate and relevant as times change, that the organization's programs and activities help to forward the mission, and that the finances and programs are monitored for accountability. In an organization that is becoming more international, finding ways to integrate international perspectives into the decision-making process so that the responsibilities of board members are carried out with these perspectives in mind is crucial.

Many different models exist for international governance structures. Three are the most common.

First, each regional area (group of chapters located close together geographically) has a board representative. A major advantage is that it ensures geographical representation. A major disadvantage is this can become cumbersome and expensive (see Chapter Eight for a further discussion of costs) as an organization grows and more board members must be added.

In a second model, specific stipulations are established for international representation on the board. This option has the advantage of some international representation but limits the size of the board by not providing one representative for each region. For example, an organization's election policies may call for a ratio such as three representatives of an eleven-member board to come from outside the United States.

The third possibility is open elections, with the nominating committee or other leadership group working to have geographical representation on the slate of candidates. The major advantages of this option are that it maintains the board at a set number of members and helps to focus the board and organization on globalism and the organization as one entity rather than distinct (geographical) constituencies. A major disadvantage is that it is dependent on the membership's voting into office a diverse group; this may or may not happen. As an organization moves along the international engagement spectrum and adopts a greater global mind-set throughout the organization, this is the most common option because it puts a premium on an integrated organization.

Dues Payments

A full spectrum exists from charging extra for the costs of servicing non-U.S. members to reducing costs to members in developing countries. There are a number of choices here, but make sure your leadership has thought out the trade-offs of each option and is making an educated policy decision.

Very early in your evolution of becoming an international membership organization, and certainly once you have chapters or affiliates outside the United States, set a consistent policy for dues payments. What groups of countries will pay what dues, and why has that amount been established? Many organizations have run into trouble when they have allowed each group of international members or chapters to negotiate an individual dues payment scheme and then, when they have too many dues schemes to manage, make them retroactively. You can avoid this problem by planning ahead at the early stages of your international growth. You may also want to set a criterion for countries that may need a temporary exemption for a currency crisis. (There is further discussion of dues and financial issues in Chapter Eleven.)

Chapter Ten

Communicating Your Messages Effectively

One of the greatest challenges for any organization, and especially those that are operating internationally, is effective communication. Words and phrases even in the same language can have different meanings for different people. We bring our culture into the words we choose, and our meaning, although it may be perfectly clear to someone from the same country or cultural background, may send a very different message or not be understood at all to someone who does not have the same background. There are some general guidelines to keep in mind when communicating in an international environment, as well as some more specific ideas for particular uses or situations.

Choosing Your Forms of Communication

Everyone has personal preferences for how they like to communicate: telephone, e-mail, fax, or letter, for example. Internationally, it is especially important to consider the vehicle that will be best received by those you are communicating with in order to generate a response and facilitate the continued exchange of communication. Depending on the situation, you should clarify directly with your correspondent (if it is a one-to-one communication) or do some research on the particular cultural norms (if you are sending something to a large group of people) regarding the most effective vehicles.

In order to choose the communication format that is most appropriate to your participants and the situation, consider some of the following questions:

- Who are the parties who are interacting (two-way communication) or the audience targeted (one-way message delivery)? Each may have its own preferred style or format.

- What needs to be communicated?

- How quickly does the communication need to take place?

- Do all the parties speak the same language, or do translations or interpretations need to be considered?

- What are the communication options available or appropriate to the situation?

- Are there budget constraints?

- Are there technology or delivery constraints regarding the message to be delivered?

General Guidelines

Once you have clarified what you hope to accomplish through your communications and the appropriate vehicles for communicating, consider some of the following guidelines.

Keep It Simple

Even those who have a working knowledge of English may not understand more complex words or phrases if English is not their native language. Simple vocabulary and sentence structures have a better chance of being understood.

Do Not Use Jargon, Acronyms, or Expressions Without Explanation

Those who share a nationality commonly use many colloquial expressions and acronyms. As familiar as they are to one group, they can be baffling for others. If you say, for example, that something has been "placed on the backburner" or it has been "approved by the EPA," do not assume that others who do not come from the United States will understand these terms. In some cases, you will still choose to use a particular expression or acronym, but with a brief explanation to make your meaning clear to your audience. The more you are conscious of your own culture and how it compares and contrasts with that of your audience, the clearer your intended messages will be.

Clarify

If you have any question as to whether you are making yourself understood, do not assume that someone understands what you are saying. Especially do not assume that silence is agreement; it can often be an indication that someone has not understood at all what you have said. In a one-on-one verbal situation, a good way to ask for confirmation is, "If I understand correctly, this means . . ." Or you can provide some choices to help determine someone's meaning: "Did you mean this or that?" With a group, you may want to ask for the group to nod their heads or raise their hands for yes or shake their head for no when you ask if they have understood what you are trying to communicate. Or if you are facilitating a session where each person's understanding and agreement is important, you can go around the room and ask each person for comments or questions. You will find your own ways of clarifying your meaning in a particular situation. The key is to realize that clarification often may be necessary.

Be Aware of Nonverbal Messages

What you are communicating and what is being communicated back to you can be embedded in what is done as much as what is being said. Pay attention to some of the nonverbal cues that you are sending and may be receiving. For example, if you are speaking with a multinational group and do not slow your speech so you can more easily be understood or you use many colloquial expressions, you may be sending the message that you do not care much about your audience or have not adequately prepared for this session. Or if someone nods at what you are saying but does not in any way respond verbally or just says yes without any additional follow-up words, that person may not be following what you are saying.

In your written communications, especially those that may accompany a verbal presentation, you might want to learn and use a foreign language translation more common to your audience to clarify a particularly complicated concept. By doing this, you send the message to your audience that you care about their understanding your message.

Be Aware of Cultural Backgrounds

Every culture has its own courtesies that send the message that you are particularly sensitive to the people you are interacting with and taboos that can hinder a relationship if you do not pay attention to them. If you are working with people from particular cultural backgrounds, take some time to learn these cultural aspects of nonverbal communication. For example, in China, it is a customary courtesy when someone hands you something such as a business card to accept it in both hands and look at it before putting it away. In some countries, written communications (even what might be considered an informal memo in the United States) must have a written signature, or it may be considered as junk mail and discarded. One organization had a majority of the organization's ballots almost discarded by many of its European members because it did not come signed by a leader of the organization.

Iris Varner and Linda Beamer in their book *Intercultural Communication in the Global Workplace* explain the necessity of doing your research before proceeding: "The blunders-and-bloops literature is full of instances where the fall was fatal and the deal came apart. It is always because someone didn't understand the why. The why is the essence of a people's culture—why people believe as they do and act as they do and give importance to things as they do. If you understand why people value some things, then you can make good guesses about why they will value other things.

Communication Reminders

- Keep your language simple.

- Avoid jargon, acronyms that are not international, and expressions that may not be clear to those who do not reside in the United States or have English as their native tongue.

- When in doubt, clarify.

- Be aware of the cultural background of those you are communicating with, and choose your words appropriately.

If you understand why they behave a certain way in one situation, you can interpret or predict behavior in other situations with a fair degree of accuracy. Once you have an insight into what people think is important and why they behave as they do, you can do business with them."[1]

Written Communication

You have more time to prepare written communications, and thus your audience will generally expect a higher standard than when you are engaging in conversation. Moreover, taking the time to know your target audience is especially important for your written messages to be well received.

Always keep what you are writing simple, and do not use jargon, acronyms, and colloquial expressions. Take the time to review your written communications (better yet, have someone from another culture or who speaks another language review it) and identify anything that is culturally based jargon or that may be particularly difficult to understand. Then see if you can substitute a simpler way of saying the same thing.

Take the time to review your written communications, identify anything that may be unclear to your target audience, and then look for substitute wording. Also think about what might be useful to international audiences. For example, include your country code when providing a telephone number or a country name in a return address. Another example is to stipulate the monetary currency you are referring to, remembering that several countries use the dollar (they include Australia and Canada), so you must specify if an amount is quoted in U.S. dollars.

Written communication gives you the time to be more aware of your nonverbal communications (and takes away some of your excuse not to have known). Look at the symbols you are using in your publications. Are they particularly U.S. centered? Do you use a lot of red, white, and blue? Consider some multicultural alternatives. It is no coincidence that the Olympic colors—black, blue, green, red, and yellow—are varied and encompass most of the colors used in country flags around the world. Colors are also important (for both positive and negative reactions) in some cultures. Remember too that seasons vary from country to country, so use month names instead. For example, July is summer in the United States and other Northern Hemisphere countries, but winter in Australia and other Southern Hemisphere countries.

Interpretation and Translation

One of the most important guidelines for your organization to keep in mind is to evaluate if and when other languages need to be used. Although translations are helpful in many situations, they may not always be necessary, and there may be more cost-effective alternatives to meet your goals.

If you do decide to use interpretation (which refers to verbal communication) or translations (in your written communications), ensure that the conversions from one language to another are of high quality. There are many sources for finding information about interpreter and translator services, but there are great variations in quality. Where possible, obtain referrals for when these services were used in situations similar to the ones you are considering. Also be aware that for many languages, there are different dialects (such as Chinese, which has many, with the two most common being Mandarin and Cantonese). Ensure that you are using the dialect that is most appropriate for your audience.

You give your interpreters or translators the best chance for success when you provide them with background regarding your organization so their translations can be accurate and culturally appropriate for your organization.

Facilitating Meetings

As your organization becomes more internationally engaged, your leadership may find itself involved in facilitating more small group sessions with participants from other countries.

Recognize that there are different cultural approaches to structuring a meeting or solving a problem, and be open to trying new approaches. Convey respect for those with different cultural approaches, and consider having participants of two different nationalities cochair the meeting. Start off with common understandings and goals to help minimize possible misunderstandings.

Seeing something in writing often makes it easier for those following a meeting in a language that is not in their native tongue. Send as many advance materials as possible. During the meeting, use handouts, overheads, PowerPoint presentations, or other written aids to supplement the verbal discussion.

Make an attempt at pronouncing the names of participants, even seemingly difficult names. You may want to write them out phonetically in advance, and do not hesitate to ask people if you are pronouncing their names correctly.

To help alleviate tension or create a bond in a smaller group, try some cross-cultural sharing techniques. Have participants share the story of their name, a short personal story, or a saying from a local elder. Storytelling is widely practiced around the world, and such stories can often reveal much about a person's approach to the world (and your meeting).

Remember not to assume that silence is agreement. Try some different approaches to encouraging participation. For example, you can go around the room at a smaller meeting and ask everyone for comments. At a large meeting, you can divide into smaller groups to encourage those not as comfortable in the language or participatory format of the meeting to participate.

Internal and External Communication

Many chapters in this book have dealt with the topic of communications within an organization, generally as well as for specific situations. In addition to the general guidelines above, see Chapter Four for communication tips for conferences or meetings, Chapter Eight for communication ideas that especially apply to multinational boards and committees, and Chapter Nine for mailings and translations for your membership. Following are some additional items you will also want to consider regarding communication with an external audience.

Research the most appropriate formats and vehicles for communicating with your target audience. You can do this by examining publications or other materials produced by other organizations that market to this audience or produced by organizations within a target country. Another way is to locate someone in your target country who can provide guidelines and suggestions for your external pieces. Remember that a publication that works well in one country or region may not work as well in another.

As your organization is becoming more international, you may want to reconsider its name. Some organizations that had names that included the word *national*, for example, found that this worked well when they were primarily focused on the United States, but as they have broadened their perspectives, this name seemed limiting. The National Society of Fundraising Executives changed its name to the Association of Fundraising Professionals in January 2001 because of international growth. Its members wanted the name to better reflect its membership that was growing throughout North America and around the world.

Be careful before you do initiate such a name change. In addition to the costs associated with such a change, such as redoing your brochures, stationery, banners, and other printed material, if you do move in the direction of some organizations and attach the word *international* to your organization's name, make sure that you are truly committed to being an international organization and that this change is not just a token gesture.

Chapter Eleven

Planning for Technical and Logistical Issues

This chapter introduces some of the technical issues you may need to address as you become more involved in an international environment. It is intended to help you identify the issues you may want to discuss with an appropriate specialist, ideally one with experience in the international arena. Nothing presented here should be seen as financial, legal, or other professional advice.

Financial Issues

In the most general terms, foreign exchange is the process of converting an amount of money in one currency to an equivalent amount in another. Changing political, economic, and social conditions throughout the world affect international markets and cause currencies to strengthen or weaken. Because these exchange rates continuously vary, planning can be a challenge.

The work you need to do to prepare your organization for foreign currency exchanges will depend on what you are trying to accomplish. Both banks and foreign exchange firms provide foreign currency exchanges as a service, and they may charge for it. If your organization is becoming involved in foreign currency exchange for the first time, consult your current financial adviser or institution as to whether it has expertise and capabilities in this area. If not, ask for a referral.

A bank that operates internationally may also be a good source for seeking the services you need. Costs and services vary, so shop around for the institution that will provide you what you need at a cost you can afford.

Many organizations find that one of the first foreign exchange issues they face is whether to accept other currencies for products and services, such as attendance at the organization's conference, or dues payments by members from outside the country. If this is the situation for your organization, first assess your staff's capacity for handling and documenting these exchanges before making a presentation to your leadership regarding options to consider. Some organizations find that accepting other currencies is a fairly easy transition. Others find it more of a challenge or especially time-consuming. A lot will depend on the expertise of your staff and any outside financial counsel or institution you are working with. Challenges may include the need for a multicurrency accounting system, opening and tracking a foreign currency account in a foreign bank, tracking currency exchange rates, and showing gains and losses from the other currencies on your financial statements.

Do your homework and be prepared. Some organizations find that a pilot project, where they begin to accept only one or two other currencies initially, such as the European euro, allows them to ascertain how they can adapt to this change without expending too many resources initially or raising expectations. The situation to avoid is pressure from a group of overseas members or others involved with your organization to make a change that you accept but cannot realistically handle.

When selling products or services overseas or holding a meeting in another country, be aware of the local tax systems. For example, you may be subject to taxes such as the value-added tax (VAT) common in many European countries.

Legal Issues

Several types of laws may apply to organizations conducting international activities. The national law of the country in which such activities are undertaken is usually the law with the most direct applicability to the organization, although state, municipal, and other local laws also may apply.

It is important for you to be aware of the laws that may apply to your organization in the countries where you have members or are conducting activities. For example, many organizations with members in Europe have discovered that Europe's privacy laws for individuals are different from those in the United States and can thus affect the way they handle members' records.

When you begin to operate internationally, determine whether your usual legal counsel has expertise in this area. If not, this person should be able to refer you to someone who can provide appropriate legal advice. A lawyer or law firm that operates internationally may be a good source for seeking professional counsel.

If you would like to acquaint yourself with issues to explore further, there are some good general sources to provide you with basic information on a country-by-country basis as to what constitutes a nonprofit organization, how they are taxed, and other relevant information. Some of these are listed in the legal resources box.

There are a few legal areas that are especially common among organizations that are operating internationally.

Legal Resources

Glassie, J. C. *International Legal Issues for Nonprofit Organizations*. Washington, D.C.: American Society of Association Executives, 1999.

United States International Grantmakers, www.usig.org or www.usig.org/countrycodes

For local conventions and visitors' bureaus: International Association of Convention and Visitors Bureaus, www.iacvb.org

Establishing and Dissolving Local Entities

If your organization is beginning to expand its operations overseas, look at the relevant local laws (national, provincial or state, municipal), finance, and tax issues for establishing a local presence. For example, in some countries, chapters can operate under their own incorporated status and in other countries only as part of the parent organization. In some countries, the enabling legislation may not exist at all for organizations like yours to operate. There may be specific laws governing how such an entity, if created locally, would be dissolved if the need to do so should arise. It is important to research these questions in advance.

Among the other questions to consider are whether local chapters can be subject to local taxes such as the VAT in Europe, whether money can be sent out of the country to pay for dues, and whether there are relevant tax treaties between the United States and the country you are dealing with that need to be considered.

Trademarks and Licensing of Name

Many organizations that have local entities in other parts of the world find they need to protect their organization's name or trademark (or both). With the increase of Web sites, this is another area where trademarks are used and organizations are finding a need to protect their interests. Laws (and the ability to enforce them) vary by country, and you should research this before making decisions about allowing your organization's name to be used in other jurisdictions.

Fundraising and Tax Deductibility

The benefits that nonprofit organizations obtain under the 501(c) section of the U.S. Internal Revenue Code are not as common in many other countries. For example, overseas donors to your organization will most likely not receive any tax deductions for their gift. And some foreign tax laws require an organization to register in the foreign jurisdiction for the donor to obtain a tax benefit. Because laws vary from country to country, research the specific situation in the countries you will be dealing with.

Privacy of Data

How you handle data obtained from members varies by law around the world. In the European Union (EU), a data privacy directive became effective in 1998 that gives citizens of EU countries certain rights to know and in some cases control how personal information about them is used. So, for example, if you publicize a membership directory and have European members, your legal counsel needs to review any specific steps you may need to take to comply with EU law.

Selling Products to Individuals in Other Countries

Circumstances that can affect the international tax picture for selling your products overseas will include whether the products or services will be sold directly or indirectly and whether sales activities (or other activities) will occur in the foreign country. Research the tax implications before becoming involved in such transactions. For an event where you sell your products while overseas, obtain information on how to return any profits to the United States.

Hotel Policies and Contracts

The issues pertaining to hotel policies and contracts in organizing meetings overseas can differ from those common with U.S. hotels. Some issues to consider are the local protocols for contract negotiations, which contract law will prevail (U.S. or local), local taxes, gratuities policies and services charges, required deposits (and in what currency), room attrition (if you have a block of rooms) and cancellation policies, and fluctuating currencies in the contract.

Clarify all costs, and get everything in writing. This is also an area where an experienced professional's counsel can be invaluable.

Overseas Employment Issues

If your operations expand to other countries in significant ways, at some stage you may consider employing staff overseas or opening an overseas office. If you are considering such a move, be aware that each country has its own labor laws (employment and severance), benefits (including holidays), taxes, and other employment policies. To make it easier to understand and deal with the employment issues they will be facing in another country, some organizations consider hiring an association management company (AMC), which for a fee hires the employee and handles these issues.

If you set up an overseas office, you will also need to consider the issues of insurance for the office, possible costs of contracting with professionals in that country to oversee accounting and legal issues, long-distance supervision of employees, and keeping these employees integrated with the headquarters staff. Another issue is salary equity: What are competitive salaries in the local market compared to within your organization, and do you want to have different rates of pay and standards within the organization?

Moving Forward

All of the issues introduced in this chapter require in-depth analysis before you make a decision on how to proceed. The intent of this chapter was to introduce some of the issues you will want to consider as part of any analysis or feasibility study that you will want to discuss with a knowledgeable professional.

Part Four

Learning from International Models

Chapter Twelve

Lessons to Be Learned from the Global Organization

Global NGOs can be classified into two categories regarding the international nature of their operations: (1) those that began in one country and expanded to other countries, generally over a significant period of years (the most common historic model), and (2) those that were founded initially as international NGOs, with representatives of a number of countries as initial founders.

Most of this book has focused on organizations in the first category that are moving along the global spectrum. For these organizations, there are often transitional phases as they expand. Initially, an organization may have a modest international program with a few projects, such as information exchanges with colleague organizations or interested individuals in other countries, a joint activity such as a conference with a colleague organization, or participation in international conferences, such as those sponsored by the United Nations. These activities have limited staffing allocations: one dedicated person or a staff member who carries the international portfolio along with other responsibilities.

This chapter looks at truly global organizations. Some have become global by moving along the international engagement spectrum, adding some of the programs described in earlier chapters of this book and now operating as a truly global organization, while others were founded globally. One of the unique aspects of a truly global organization is having as a priority the goal of treating its members and operations in all parts of the world equally. To fulfill this goal, global organizations need to structure their operations in ways that will meet the variety of expectations and needs of a global constituency.

The following sections examine areas that can be seen in varying degrees in organizations as they move along the international engagement spectrum and are a priority for global organizations. They play out in ways that can provide useful lessons to organizations at various stages in the internationalization process.

Organizational Structure

No matter what structure your organization might choose, to function as a single organization, there must be some unifying ties, usually resting with a headquarters operation. Except in rare circumstances, the headquarters operation (no matter how weak), will be located within the boundaries of one nation. As an organization becomes more global, however, and increasing numbers of other countries are involved, inevitably there is more pressure on the headquarters to allow greater variations in the local units. The global organization must balance these competing pressures, determining which issues are core values for the organization that all of its local entities must subscribe to, which operating procedures must be standardized, and where local variances can occur.

While historically many international NGOs (as was also the case in the private sector) had highly centralized structures, current trends appear to be toward more local autonomy. Dennis Young noted in an article in *Voluntas* that of three organizations he looked at, "two of the three associations [considered] are moving toward a more decentralised structure with greater emphasis on local and regional concerns and on the autonomy and diversity of local affiliates. The direction in which the [third] will move as it expands its international programme is unclear."[1]

CIVICUS is an international alliance dedicated to strengthening citizen action and civil society throughout the world and a model for many NGOs around the world. Founded in 1993 as a global organization with a multinational board of directors, the operating processes that CIVICUS has developed have often been seen as models for other NGOs operating internationally.

In its initial stages, CIVICUS focused on maintaining its global character by developing a regional structure that would give each region representatives who would have a role in the organization's decision making. As the organization evolved, it continued to discuss the most effective way to maintain its globalism and operate as a global organization. Although the commitment to global diversity was maintained and strengthened, the focus on regions was made more flexible and left more open to each region's own choice.

A decade after its founding in 1993, CIVICUS said this about its focus on regions: "As part of its global character, CIVICUS has established a regional presence under a variety of structures, depending on what the CIVICUS members in each region feel would be most helpful in strengthening civil society and its organizations. This regional presence serves as a communication point with civil society organizations, the business sector and government. Regional-specific programme initiatives are also being developed based on the global CIVICUS programme areas."[2] In addition, CIVICUS decentralized its operations, moving from a secretariat based in Washington, D.C., to one based in Johannesburg, South Africa, with additional advocacy and program offices in London and Washington, D.C.

The Oxfam International confederation created in the mid-1990s is an example of a new model that some international NGOs are trying. Although Oxfam affiliates have existed for a number of years in several countries, it was only in the mid-1990s that these national groups decided to strengthen their affiliation by founding Oxfam International and working more closely in areas such as advocacy work, program harmonization, and emergency response. Oxfam affiliates collectively govern Oxfam International, set policy and create plans, and manage the resulting activities in ways that create effective alignment of their work, resources, and policies. Affiliates take independent responsibility for allocating resources and managing their work.

To maintain its decentralization and sense of globalism, Oxfam was incorporated in the Netherlands; it set up a small secretariat in Oxford, England, U.K., and advocacy offices in Brussels, Belgium, and Washington, D.C., U.S.A. As it evolved, it developed a particularly versatile structure adaptable to the ongoing change it sees in the international environment. An early strategic plan stated, "We are 12 autonomous organizations, each with its own history and supporters, but we nevertheless share a distinctive profile based on a combination of four approaches [or core values]." Oxfam International aims to model its concept of global citizenship by focusing on extending its cooperative efforts in alliances and networks to working relationships with other NGOs, international organizations, and the corporate sector. It has also created a variety of ways in which other organizations can be associated with it. In addition to the member affiliates, there are categories such as policy associates (organizations with which Oxfam International will consult at the board level on major policy issues), provisional members (organizations that share Oxfam's values and mission but participate selectively in governance and activities), and Oxfam groups (groups of individuals who support individual Oxfams or Oxfam International as a whole through campaigning, fundraising, and other forms of activism).

Lessons on Structure

- The more parts of the world in which an organization has interactions or activities, the more it will want to determine which practices need to be standardized among its local entities or partners and which can vary or be locally customized.

- The larger an organization's international presence is, the more flexible it should be in looking at options for its operations.

- Organizations that want to grow internationally and develop sustainable structures are willing to review their progress in relation to their organizational goals and make modifications as needed.

Communication

As the organization grows internationally, its headquarters organization needs to work harder at continuing to develop and provide effective communication mechanisms. An important challenge for organizations that are truly committed to all members throughout the world is to look after the interest of members or constituents who are not residents of the headquarters' nation or are citizens of countries where communications can be a challenge in a way that is equitable to those that are more accessible. An organization that is truly striving to operate as an international entity will make this one of its priorities, with its goals being operations that could be transferred to any other part of the world and not change dramatically. How an organization functions in reality will generally be somewhere along a spectrum.

Iris Varner and Linda Beamer in their book *Intercultural Communication in the Global Workplace* note, "The first step in effective intercultural communication is the [understanding and] acceptance of diversity."[3] This understanding, which does not come easily to many people, is essential within a global organization.

As organizations become more global, it is increasingly important to determine appropriate and effective internal communication vehicles. Geographical distance and national political boundaries often constrain delivery options. At the same time, with the introduction of mass technology to many homes and offices around the world, the expectations of all members, regardless of location, have increased, particularly regarding speed of communication.

Global organizations make the commitment to mitigate the disadvantages to members or constituents who are in countries where technology may not be as accessible, communication costs are higher, or English (often an operational language for the organization) is not common.

Zonta International is a service organization dedicated to improving the status of women, with members in over sixty-five countries and a multinational board. Zonta has had presidents who have come from countries with communication constraints and where the costs of ongoing communications with the U.S.-based headquarters have been costly. Nevertheless, the organization believes that it has a commitment to maintaining equitable access and has budgeted the costs of absorbing this communication. It also conducts ongoing reviews of its delivery service to its worldwide members.

The International Society for Third-Sector Research (ISTR) promotes research and education in the fields of philanthropy, civil society, and the nonprofit sector with a multinational board and membership. It has made a commitment to a broad-based communication network through a number of vehicles. Its publications and papers from its conferences are available in Spanish and French on its Web site, as well as English, and its journal, *Voluntas,* has abstracts in French, German, and Spanish. ISTR's leadership has also considered adding Arabic, Japanese, and Korean translations of *Voluntas* to attract and retain members who primarily use those languages. To increase accessibility, ISTR has made its publications available on-line to subscribers as well as in a printed format. In addition, all of its meetings (annual conference and board and committee meetings) are rotated to different venues around the world to make them accessible to its board members and the general membership. At its biennial conferences, the plenary sessions are translated into French and Spanish, and one paper session in every time slot is also translated into these languages.

When CIVICUS moved its headquarters from the United States to South Africa, it hired new staff and set up operations in the new host country. Yet with its commitment to communicate with its members and global NGO constituency, it continued to maintain its weekly e-mail newsletters and other communications with its members in a nearly seamless way during this physical transition.

The International Society for the Prevention of Child Abuse and Neglect (ISPCAN), founded in 1977 to support individuals and organizations working to protect children worldwide from abuse and neglect, is a global interdisciplinary organization with nearly seventeen hundred members in 120 countries and a multinational board of directors. As a relatively small organization in terms of budget and staff size, ISPCAN has become particularly creative in developing internal communication mechanisms. In addition to designing its Web site as an "International Web Membership Community" so that members from different countries have easy access to information, it has initiated a listserv, a searchable Web-based membership directory, and a virtual issues discussion (VID) forum.

For the VID, held biannually, the ISPCAN leadership designates an expert faculty that decides on a topic. A facilitator, who is also an expert on the issue, writes a relevant paper for the membership. Three additional faculty panelists are selected to represent views and experiences in other countries and disciplines, and they also post initial papers or perspectives. The VID is promoted in advance to members as a seventy-two-hour virtual discussion on a specific topic, with access to information so they may download materials and participate in or observe the discussions. The facilitator and panelists are each active on a "daily" basis throughout different time zones to assist and respond. Following the VID, the facilitator provides a paper integrating information from the discussion, enhanced by the international and interdisciplinary experiences shared throughout the process, and offers this to the members as a listserv message.

ISPCAN uses the same international participation process in the development of fact sheets and guidelines and other membership services, including case studies, in its newsletter. Internally, within eight years, ISPCAN has evolved from needing to support the purchase of modems and provide e-mail training for ISPCAN board members to the practice of posting committee reports and council meeting board books on a council intranet page for councillors on every continent to download for review prior to board meetings, making the information more timely and the process more cost-effective. These vehicles supplement the one face-to-face council meeting budgeted per year.

Lessons on Communications

- The more widespread an organization's operations become, the more attention its staff and leaders will need to pay, and the more time they will need to devote, to developing effective internal communication mechanisms.

- Thinking strategically and creatively about communications options can help an organization identify which types of communications are the most cost-effective in any given situation.

- Although cost-effective means can often be found, the organization committed to serving all members or constituents equally, wherever they may reside, may need to budget adequate funds to carry out this goal in practice.

Special Staffing Considerations

The staff of international NGOs have the special challenge of working with people and organizations of different cultures, ethnicities, nationalities, and religions. Although some of the training and skills they need have been discussed in Chapter Two, it is essential that staff in global organizations receive ongoing skills training and that these capabilities be institutionalized into its operations.

A preliminary list of skills helpful to the staff of an international NGO includes international outlook and knowledge; multicultural sensitivities; a philosophy of remaining neutral among members of differing cultures, nationalities, and political perspectives; and communication and facilitation skills that will help bring about and implement consensus.

Many organizations are now placing increased attention on diversifying their professional staff members to better represent a diversified membership. Having a multicultural staff that is encouraged to work together can model effective behavioral patterns for the entire organization.

As part of its headquarters move to Johannesburg, CIVICUS undertook a large expansion in its staff that has resulted in a diverse and multinational staff profile. The eighteen full-time staff and interns in the Johannesburg office in 2003 came from ten countries: New Zealand, Uganda, Luxembourg, South Africa, the United States, Wales, England, Germany, Canada, and the Philippines. Thus, CIVICUS has used its hiring practices to build a global perspective into the organizational structure.

A diverse staff can come with challenges as well as benefits. In his book *Inside NGOs*, Naoki Suzuki talks about how different standards of leadership can be a challenge for the multinational staff. One example he gives is of the approach most common in the training of many American and other Western leaders: the "player-coach"—willing to listen to the ideas of their staff members and do what they tell others to do. In many African and Asian countries, however, it can be more common for leaders to be set apart and held in higher esteem. Being part of the team can weaken the leadership image.[4]

Organizations with staff spread around the world should place a special focus on fostering good ongoing communication and coordination between this staff and the headquarters staff. The CIVICUS leadership endeavors to involve as many staff as possible in its meetings, external representation work, other organizations' conferences and events, and meetings with partner and member organizations so that they share the same learning experiences about the organization and periodically meet face to face.

Chapter Thirteen

Comparative Examples from Other Countries

Although most of the examples in this book are of U.S. organizations that have increased their international engagement, similar patterns apply to organizations throughout the world. The examples in this chapter illustrate that the challenges faced, and the lessons learned, by locally or nationally based organizations that are looking to engage internationally are similar (although of course not identical) wherever in the world these organizations may originate or operate. (This chapter may be particularly helpful to readers from outside the United States, who may wonder if the suggestions and trends explored so far are applicable in other parts of the world.)

Clean Up Australia, Then the World

Clean Up the World was created in 1992 as an extension of the successful Clean Up Australia campaign, initiated in 1989 by Australian builder and sailor Ian Kiernan. Kiernan completed a solo race around the world in 1986–1987 and resolved to do something about the growing problem of polluted waterways. Starting with a massive clean-up of Sydney Harbor and expanding to incorporate projects throughout Australia, volunteers worked together in their own communities to carry out local clean-up activities, uniting with like-minded groups in other geographical locations.

The hands-on nature of the activity helped lead to its success in Australia. With the publicity that Clean Up Australia received, those associated with the event began to receive inquiries from other parts of the world and embassies based in Australia. The small staff of Clean Up Australia spent a year researching the possibilities for expanding Clean Up Australia internationally by writing to organizations that had contacted them and learning about environmental networks. They were also approached by the United Nations Environment Program (UNEP) about possible global sponsorship, a partnership that eventually became one of the keys to the initial success of Clean Up the World.

The initial development funding for Clean Up the World was provided by UNEP in 1992 and matched by the U.S.-based EGBAR Foundation. Some of the initial UNEP funding was used to produce a brochure that communicated the message in easy-to-understand language. The brochure was produced in English, French, and Spanish and was sent free of charge to interested groups and networks. The concept the group communicated was, "We have been successful in Australia, and we would be happy to share what we have learned to take the 'Think Globally, Act Locally' concept to the next stage."

After two years of development and planning, the inaugural Clean Up the World event took place in 1993, with volunteers around the world working on the same day in their local communities to carry out local clean-up activities. It exceeded all expectations and involved an estimated 30 million people in 80 countries. By 1995, volunteers in 110 countries were represented. Clean Up the World is looking at future growth and how its organizational structure can best reflect the international nature of its first successful years.

The success of Clean Up the World can be attributed to a number of factors:

- A popular idea at an opportune time
- Obtaining an initial funding base
- Collaboration with other groups to expand the leverage of limited resources (early partners included the Girl and Boy Guides)

- Local groups in other countries to spearhead and be responsible for the local activity in those regions
- Attention to public relations

Clean Up the World's successful evolution from Clean Up Australia was aided by some strategic leadership about what they envisioned Clean Up the World to be so that its growth would be by design, and not just be reacting to interest expressed from around the world.

KidLink

KidLink was the idea of Odd de Presno, from Norway, in 1990. He was involved in facilitating on-line discussions among adults in Europe and, inspired by his daughter, wanted to expand this dialogue to include children. The first on-line discussion was organized during a Children's Cultural Week in 1990 in Arendal, Norway, with several participants from ages seven to sixteen. Later that year, a group of teachers associated with the Science and Technology Network for People in Education in Canada enthusiastically joined the movement, and a discussion was organized that also included children from Canada and the United States. The focus was simple, with responses to four basic questions: (1) Who am I? (2) What do I want the world to be like when I grow up? (3) What can I do now to make the world a better place when I grow up? and (4) What can I do now to make this happen?

As KidLink continued to evolve, its founders' emphasis was to involve as many children as possible. To do this in a culturally sensitive way, KidLink's leadership provided a number of options for involvement appropriate to children in different countries. Although the main means of collecting the responses was through global electronic computer conferencing, other means of communication were used where access to computer conferencing is difficult for technical, economic, or other reasons. Children were also encouraged to visualize their vision in some way that was comfortable to them, for example, by making a drawing or using computer graphics or a making videotape. And although the initial language of KidLink was English, languages were added as the project's participation grew in different parts of the world. KidLink has used a number of options for maintaining its electronic network, at various times being hosted by different institutional or corporate computers and Internet servers.

Enforcing the concept that personal contact is important even in the age of fast and efficient electronic communication, KidLink began to bring together its program coordinators for training and organize conferences for its on-line discussion participants. And as its participants and program grew, KidLink professionalized its management and created an international board of directors. Ten years after its initial forum, KidLink had a global span with eighty-six public mailing lists administered by an organization of some five hundred volunteers from forty-two countries, with the work coordinated through a private mailing list on its own host computer network. Its activities are conducted in nineteen languages and through a multilingual Web site. A KidLink museum was also opened in Norway.

KidLink has augmented its resources by publicizing its activities, entering competitions, and winning numerous awards for its efforts. For example, an Internet server was donated to it as an award for a contest on student Internet innovations. It also seeks to expand its impact by inviting other NGOs to become partners in its work.

Shanghai Women's Federation

Although governmentally sponsored, the Shanghai Women's Federation operates in many of the same ways as NGOs in the Western world. With a mission to improve the status of women (through the "four selves" of self-respect, self-confidence, self-reliance, and self-improvement), it works on issues such as education and training, the prevention of domestic violence, and sponsoring neighborhood legal aid and health centers.

With the opening-up period of China and the transformation to developing a market economy starting in the 1990s, the Shanghai Women's Federation developed networks to expand its contacts with those from other countries that could be helpful in meeting its own local goals. It established working relationships with women's organizations in the United States, the Netherlands, Japan, Norway, Brazil, Austria, Germany, Bulgaria, South Korea, Thailand, and Mynamar. Its representatives attend regional and international meetings, and invited leaders from around the world discuss issues from joint ventures among businesswomen to the gathering of gender-based statistics to help with policymaking. The foundation has also initiated some joint projects with organizations in the United States and Germany on women's training programs.

Conclusion

As the successful internationalization of the organizations in this chapter demonstrate, the concept of strategically increasing the international engagement of a locally based organization (Clean Up Australia and the Shanghai Women's Federation) or idea (children's on-line discussions) is similar throughout the world. Locally or nationally based organizations, wherever they may start, can take the ideas described in this book and, by customizing them to their own situation, find them relevant. The basic process of taking an organization international by focusing on its own strengths, taking advantage of opportunities that present themselves, staying focused, and proceeding deliberately toward shared goals can be found as the basis for successful programs in organizations throughout the world that are now engaging internationally.

Chapter Fourteen

Looking Forward

If your organization is already moving along the spectrum of international engagement in strategic ways or is poised to do so, it is at the forefront of a movement that will strengthen the role that nonprofit organizations can play to improve the world in the years ahead.

As you move along the spectrum or stay internationally engaged at a comfortable point for your organization on the spectrum, continue to be strategic in your thinking and planning. Regularly review where along the spectrum you are heading or remaining, why you have chosen that point or target, and how to maintain the needed commitment. All of your stakeholders must understand why this international engagement makes sense to the organization and continue to develop their own global awareness. Only when you know where you are headed and why, can you choose the activities and tools that will best help you to get there.

Organizations that are engaging internationally need to anticipate, assess, and respond to a continuously changing world. Reviewing past trends can provide some clues to the future. What are some of the emerging trends you might want to anticipate? For example, as more countries increase their governmental connections with the rest of the world (for example, the expansion of membership countries into multilateral organizations such as the European Community and the World Trade Organization), they will face increasing global pressure to be more transparent regarding their domestic policies that affect others around the world and to provide enabling legislation and government-sanctioned roles to the nongovernmental sector. Thus, growth in the nongovernmental sector around the world can be expected to continue. This growth will provide a larger array of options (and challenges to navigate) for international engagement. It will also provide more potential partners for locally or nationally based organizations that would like to become more connected to the broader international nonprofit community.

Some of the technologies that were referred to by authors writing about international communications ten years ago as being critical to successful communications, such as fax machines and worldwide messenger services, are now almost obsolete, overtaken by e-mail and Web sites where information can be sent or posted almost instantaneously. It would not be surprising for this technological progression to continue and for some of the technologies mentioned in this book to also become obsolete (perhaps by the time you are reading this a few years after its publication). This technological progress will continue to bring with it greater options (and generally a corresponding decrease in cost) to organizations in communicating internationally. But the greater lesson may be that these technologies are just tools that will change over time; the concepts and ideas of inclusiveness, cultural sensitivity, and understanding the human aspects of international engagement are critical to master and longer lasting.

Although in many countries around the world, including the United States, the role of volunteers will continue to be important to nonprofit organizations, the trend toward professionalization of staffs and operations can be expected to grow. In addition, the support of capacity-building initiatives for the nongovernmental sector by governments, private foundations, and other donors can be expected to continue. This may result in a continued increase in the abilities and sophistication of the sector and mean that the expectations of potential partner groups around the world will also be greater. Thus, there will be a greater need to research potential partners and networks before you commit to them.

These trends may or may not come to pass, but outlining some predictions does point to a process that your organization should undertake as you continue your international engagement: reviewing the international events and trends around you and assessing how they will affect or can be influenced by your organization. So venture forth: be creative and strategic in your thinking and planning, and your organization's own culture and strengths will take you in the direction best suited to your own challenges and needs.

Notes

Preface

1. *Nongovernmental organizations* (NGOs) is the term most commonly used internationally for organizations that are not governmental or part of the corporate sector. The term most commonly used in the United States is *nonprofit organization*. Because most of the examples in this book come from the United States, I use *nonprofit organization* or just the more generic *organization* most often throughout the book. There are numerous other terms used to describe this third sector (neither governmental nor private), and this breadth of terminology can be confusing. See the Glossary at the end of this book for the variety of terms used to describe the sector and how they are most commonly used.

2. H. Anheier, M. Glasius, and M. Kaldor, eds., *Global Civil Society 2002* (Oxford: Oxford University Press, 2002), p. 3.

3. United Nations, *The Four Global Women's Conferences, 1975–1995: Historical Perspective* (New York: United Nations, May 2000).

4. United Nations, *The Four Global Women's Conferences, 1975–1995: Historical Perspective* (New York: United Nations, May 2000).

5. K. Annan, speech to the Fiftieth Annual DPI/NGO Conference, "Building Partnerships," Sept. 10, 1997.

Chapter One

1. I. C. Stewart to the author, e-mail, May 2003.

Chapter Four

1. Chicago Foundation for Women newsletter, Winter 2002, pp. 4–5.

Chapter Eight

1. H. V. Perlmutter, "The Torturous Evolution of the Multinational Company," *Columbia Journal of World Business*, 1969.

Chapter Ten

1. I. Varner and L. Beamer, *Intercultural Communication in the Global Workplace* (Boston: Irwin, 1995), p.2.

Chapter Twelve

1. D. Young, "Organising Principles for International Advocacy Associations," *Voluntas*, 1992, 2(1), 1–28.
2. CIVICUS. [www.civicus.org].
3. I. Varner and L. Beamer, *Intercultural Communication in the Global Workplace* (Boston: Irwin, 1995), p. xiii.
4. N. Suzuki, *Inside NGOs: Learning to Manage Conflicts Between Headquarters and Field Offices* (London: Intermediate Technology Publications, 1998).

Glossary

Association A membership organization of individuals or companies sharing common goals. Most commonly used to refer to professional societies and trade associations.

Charitable organization Most often used for nonprofit organizations in the United Kingdom and many other Commonwealth countries. Sometimes also used in the United States to describe nonprofit organizations focused most directly on charitable activities.

Civil society organization A term developed to move away from defining an organization by what it is not (nonprofit, nongovernmental) toward a focus on what it is—in this case, organizations with a focus on the greater good of society.

Global Pertaining to countries in several different regions around the world. Although sometimes *international* and *global* are used interchangeably, *global* is often used to refer to an organization that has activities or operations throughout the world. It may also be an organization that has made a commitment to having a multinational focus and decision-making apparatus, widening its international focus and operations beyond its home country.

Independent sector organization A term that seeks to differentiate the group of organizations that are independent of the governmental sector.

International Pertaining to two or more countries. Although sometimes *international* and *global* are used interchangeably, *international* is often used to refer to an organization that is beginning to extend itself to other countries or that operates in a few countries but not necessarily worldwide. Although it conducts activities or has members in other countries, it retains a major focus on its home country.

Nongovernmental organization The most commonly used term internationally to refer to nonprofit organizations. It evolved from the United Nations practice of identifying certain organizations as being nongovernmental.

Nonprofit organization The most commonly used term in the United States to refer to these organizations. It evolved from the tax status of these organizations as not making a profit for their owners or shareholders (such as a business does) and thus being entitled to certain tax exemptions.

Private voluntary organization Development organizations or those that provide social support such as humanitarian assistance.

Professional society A membership organization that represents individuals having a profession or trade in common.

Social sector organization Like *civil society organization*, a term that focuses on the greater good of society that many of these organizations hope to foster through their missions.

Third-sector organization A term developed to differentiate organizations that are neither governmental nor corporate and thus belong to a third sector.

Trade association A membership organization that represents a group of companies having a business or trade in common. In most countries where this type of association exists, its members and board of directors are volunteers, and the organization may hold a legal status similar to other nonprofit organizations.

Voluntary organization Because many nonprofit organizations operate with a high level of volunteer involvement, this term is sometimes used to describe organizations in the nonprofit sector as well.

Bibliography

International Engagement and Cultural Understanding

Anheier, H., Glasius, M., and Kaldor, M., eds. *Global Civil Society 2002*. Oxford: Oxford University Press, 2002.

Axtell, R. E. (ed.). *Do's and Taboos Around the World*. New York: Wiley, 1985.

Culture Shock! series. Singapore: Times Editions Pte Ltd.

Culturegram series, Brigham Young University, David M. Kennedy Center for International Studies, Provo, Utah, USA (four-page country write-up available for over 110 countries), www.culturegrams.com.

Florini, A. (ed.). *The Third Force: The Rise of Transnational Civil Society*. Washington, D.C.: Carnegie Endowment for International Peace, 2000.

Goman, C. K. *Managing in a Global Organization*. Menlo Park, Calif.: Crisp Publications, 1994.

Koenig, B. "The Management of International Non-Governmental Organizations in the 1990s." *Transnational Associations*, 1996, 2, 66–72.

Koenig, B. "The Fine Art of Planning an International Meeting." *Nonprofit World*, Nov.–Dec. 1998, pp. 12–13.

Koenig, B. "Is It Time for You to Go International?" *Nonprofit World*, May–June 1998, pp. 13–15.

Koenig, B. "The Benefits of a Global Perspective." *Journal of Volunteer Administration*, Spring 2000, pp. 43–46.

Koenig, B. "How Relevant Is Global Thinking?" *Nonprofit World*, Jan.–Feb. 2001, pp. 17–18.

Mead, R. "International Management: Cross Cultural Dimensions." In R. Rosen, P. Digh, M. Singer, and C. Phillips (eds.), *Global Literacies: Lessons on Business, Leadership and National Cultures*. Cambridge, Mass.: Blackwell, 2000.

Suzuki, N. *Inside NGOs: Learning to Manage Conflicts Between Headquarters and Field Offices*. London: Intermediate Technology Publications, 1998.

Svevo-Cianci, K. *Associations and the Global Marketplace*. Washington, D.C.: American Society of Association Executives, 1995.

Varner, I., and Beamer, L. *Intercultural Communication in the Global Workplace*. Burr Ridge, Ill.: Irwin, 1995.

Young, D. "Organising Principles for International Advocacy Associations." *Voluntas: International Journal of Voluntary and Nonprofit Organizations*, 1992, 2(1), 1–28.

Young, D., Koenig, B., Najam, A., and Fisher, J. "Strategy and Structure in Managing Global Associations." *Voluntas: International Journal of Voluntary and Nonprofit Organizations*, 1999, 10(4), 323–341.

Strategic Planning

Barry, B. *Strategic Planning Workbook for Nonprofit Organizations*. St. Paul, Minn.: Amherst Wilder Foundation, 1997.

Drucker Foundation/Jossey-Bass. Drucker Foundation Self-Assessment Tool. USA www.pfdf.org or www.josseybass.com, 1999.

Kaye, J., and Allison, M. *Strategic Planning for Nonprofit Organizations*. San Francisco: Jossey-Bass, 1997.

Web Sites

These Web sites were functional as of 2003, but there is a possibility that they have been discontinued or moved by their owners.

Centre for the Study of Global Governance, London School of Economics, www.lse.ac.uk/Depts/global/Yearbook/yearbook.htm. The annual *Global Civil Society* yearbook.

CIVICUS, www.civicus.org. A global network of NGOs. The Web site provides information on international trends affecting the NGO community.

Global Opportunities, www.asaenet.org/go. Provides basic information for organizations that are operating internationally.

Going International, www.goinginternational.com. Provides information and resources for organizations that are operating internationally.

Idealist, www.idealist.org. A directory of NGOs around the world, many of them looking for partners.

Index